GODIFY

God's Top 10 Songs

T. K. Anderson

ENTRUSTED MINISTRIES

Connecting your Story with God's Story

Scottsdale, Arizona

Published by Entrusted Ministries
Scottsdale, Arizona (USA)

Acknowledgments:
Editing: Daniel Johnson, Barbara Conley
Interior Design: Karen Stuart, Susie Untalan
Cover Design: David Landis

©2024, T.K. Anderson Godify: God's Top 10 Songs

First edition: March 2024

Printed in the United States of America

To my incredible wife, Dee,

You're the beat to my heart and a melody to my soul. As I contemplate God's playlist, I couldn't help but think of you and the beautiful music you bring into my life every day.

Your love and support have guided me in this exploration of God's songs. You've been a rock and inspiration. Like a perfect harmony, you've filled every moment of this journey with warmth and joy.

Thank you for being a constant source of love and inspiration. This book is a tribute to God's timeless melodies and a tribute to our time together. Here's to many more chapters filled with laughter, love, and music.

With all my love,

-T.K.

CONTENTS

6-22-24
Started reading

Introduction

What if God had a Spotify Playlist? What would it look like? At Compass Church we explored that question in a series that became the book you are reading. We looked at ten songs that bring music to the soul. I can hear someone asking, did God write music in the Bible? What, you didn't know God was a songwriter? Interestingly enough, He is. In fact, God wrote 150 songs. You may not know this, but the Book of Psalms is an entire collection of songs inspired by God for the people of God.

God enjoys music so much He surrounds Himself with it. He knows how important it is to us as well. Music has the power to draw us away from God or to lead us to Him. Music evokes deep emotions and longing, transcends thought and language, and has the power to reach inside us and touch our soul. We join in with music by singing.

The purpose of singing in worship goes beyond entertainment or personal expression. It takes us from a me-centered mindset into one of entering the presence of God. Or in the case of a music leader, it takes a crowd and turns it into one voice singing for an audience of one. Music serves as a ministry to the church by creating an atmosphere where we encounter God's presence and open ourselves up to the leading of the Holy Spirit. Singing unites us as worshippers and fosters a sense of community and shared commitment. It allows us to engage with the words of the song, internalize the truths being sung, and respond to God's love and faithfulness.

From the Old Testament to the New Testament, singing is highlighted to honor God and call out His greatness. The Psalms in particular are filled with songs of praise and worship, with King David setting a precedent for the importance of singing in worship.

The New Testament also emphasizes the significance of singing with Jesus and His disciples singing hymns during the Last Supper, and Paul encouraging believers to sing psalms, hymns, and spiritual songs.

God's music involves both praise and worship. Praise is an expression of approval or admiration. We can sing our praise, shout it, dance it. Worship involves adoration, reverence and humility. It is an attitude of humility and reverence that connects us to God. Inspired music combines these forces by engaging our lips, ears, hands and feet in stating or singing our praises then coming close to God with our hearts.

The Bible provides glimpses into God's appreciation of music. In the Old Testament, Zephaniah 3:17 says, *"The Lord your God is in your midst, a Mighty One who will save. He will rejoice over you with gladness; He will quiet you by His love; He will exult over you with loud singing."* So, God not only delights in the presence of His people, but also expresses His joy through singing.

In 1 Samuel 16:14-23, we are introduced to a young man who played a lyre or small harp for Saul, the King of Israel. He was a shepherd who had just been anointed in a private ceremony by the prophet Samuel. Immediately afterward, King Saul became melancholy and anxious. Acting on the advice of his servants, he sent out messengers to seek a musician to help cheer him up.

David played for the king and found favor in his eyes. Because of his musical talent he was appointed Saul's arms-bearer and was tasked with playing for the king to cheer him up whenever the need arose.

Eventually David would become king himself. He wrote nearly half of the songs that make up the book of Psalms. He was known for dancing before God and had no concern for what others thought of him when he was celebrating.

Music was of the highest importance in Israelite worship, as is clear from many parts of the Old Testament, notably the Psalms.

In 1 Chronicles 25:1 it says, *"David chose those who were to be charge of music. They were to praise the Lord by playing cymbals, harps and other stringed instruments."* They were choosy about their playlist.

The Levitical musicians' role in leading and directing worship was crucial, for it was they who encouraged the people to worship God with conviction, harmony, and vitality. David's organization prepared for the Levites' leading of worship in Solomon's temple, as illustrated by the temple dedication service when the great Levitical orchestra and choir made their declaration: *"He is good; His love endures forever."* (2 Chronicles 5:12-14; 7:1-6; cf. 1 Chr. 15-16)

In the New Testament, the apostle Paul encourages believers

to express their gratitude and praise to God through music. Ephesians 5:19-20 advises, *"addressing one another in psalms and hymns and spiritual songs, singing and making melody to the Lord with your heart, giving thanks always and for everything to God the Father in the name of our Lord Jesus Christ."* This verse emphasizes the transformative power of music in fostering a sense of closeness with God and expressing heartfelt gratitude.

The Book of Psalms, often referred to as the hymnbook of the Bible, stands as a testament to the role of music in worship. Comprising 150 poems or songs, Psalms covers a wide range of human emotions and experiences, expressing praise, lament, thanksgiving, and supplication – earnest prayers. Many of the Psalms were originally composed as songs, reflecting the diverse ways in which believers can approach God through music.

Various types of psalms are found in the book, each serving a unique purpose. For instance, psalms of praise, such as Psalm 100, exhort believers to celebrate and acknowledge the greatness of God. In times of trouble, psalms of lament, such as Psalm 13, provide a framework for expressing grief and seeking God's comfort. Additionally, psalms of thanksgiving, like Psalm 136, underscore the importance of gratitude in our relationship with God.

The Psalms encompass a wide range of human emotions and musical expressions, illustrating the varied nature of human experience. By including these diverse psalms, the Bible acknowledges the profound impact music can have on the spirit and its potential to facilitate a deeper relationship with God.

Godify

Today music has evolved beyond the confines of a cultural or sacred space. The advent of streaming services, such as Spotify, has revolutionized how individuals access and experience music on a global scale. The statistics surrounding these platforms offer insights into the significance of music in people's lives.

As of the latest available data, Spotify has over 345 million active users worldwide, with more than 155 million subscribers enjoying premium services. iTunes and the iPod revolutionized the music industry in the early 2000s, as the hardware and software which popularized singles over albums and allowed users to store thousands of songs on one device. The company was slow to get in on the streaming business, but once they did, their subscriber count grew rapidly. Their song library now has over 100 million songs.

These staggering numbers reflect the role music plays in our culture. The diversity of genres and the accessibility of music through streaming services echo the desire to connect with emotions and get the mood boost music provides. The German philosopher, Karl Marx, was quoted as saying, "Religion is the opium of the people." If he were living today, he might consider changing that to "Music is the opium of the people."

Singing our prayers makes it possible to articulate our thoughts, emotions, and heartfelt prayers in an expressive manner. Singing prayers, whether individually or collectively, transforms the act of communication with God into a dynamic and participatory experience.

Living in an attitude of worship through music extends beyond Sunday services. Worship involves all our lives and not just singing. Our playlist of songs and thoughts sets the backdrop of our lives and helps determine what we do. It all starts with cultivating a mindfulness and awareness of God throughout the day. Whispering a prayer in the busyness and chaos. Being aware that *"In Him we live and move and have our being."* (Acts 17:28) It is called practicing the presence of God. Colossians 3:16 encourages believers to, *"Let the Word of Christ dwell in you richly, teaching and admonishing one another in all wisdom, singing psalms and hymns and spiritual songs, with thankfulness in your hearts to God."* This verse emphasizes the integration of music into everyday living as a means of nurturing a constant awareness of God's presence.

As we navigate streaming services like Spotify, the importance of music in our lives mirrors the timeless connection between us and God. The statistics on global music consumption attest to the enduring significance of music as a universal language.

Ultimately, living in an attitude of worship involves recognizing God's presence in the ordinary moments of life. Whether singing prayers, listening to sacred compositions, or engaging in worship with other believers, music becomes a conduit to express what we are feeling and connect with God. Are you ready to sing along with God's songs for your life? Let's get to it.

Chapter 1

Hello Fear, It's Me and God

Psalm 91

The Old Testament Book of Psalms is a gateway for us into the historical context of how God interacted with His people thousands of years ago and how those same interactions still make sense in our lives today. The Book of Psalms is rich in content, wisdom, and application. It will surprise you because at its core it is about the human experience. As much as we want to think we live in amazing (or different/modern) times, which we do, the truth is that human nature and our struggles in life are as old as humanity.

Before we dive in let me provide a little background. The Book of Psalms is a compilation of hymns or poems in Hebrew. In the Bible there are 150 Psalms. The book is divided into five parts with each section concluding with a doxology which is a hymn of praise. The Psalms come in various forms, including songs of praise, public and individual lamentations, royal Psalms, and imprecatory prayers (Psalms in which the author calls down calamity, destruction, and God's anger and judgment on His enemies). Also, there are Psalms of individual and public thanksgiving, wisdom, pilgrimage, and other categories. The Psalms give credit to King David and other figures in the Bible, such as Asaph, the sons of Korah, Moses, and Solomon.

Where does it get its name? In English, the title of the book comes from the Greek term ψαλμοί (psalmoi), which implies "instrumental music" and the words that accompany it. The book's Hebrew name, Tehillim (תהילים), means "praises." The word Psalm means song or praise. The entire book is plural and is called The Book of Psalms. While each one of the 150 chapters is singular, as in Psalm 23, Psalm 51, or Psalm 119.

What does the Book of Psalms teach us about God and our relationship with Him? C. S. Lewis once commented that "the Psalms are poems, and poems intended to be sung: not doctrinal treatises, nor even sermons." [1] Although I agree with Lewis that the Psalms are not doctrinal conversations, the Psalms do teach a ton of great doctrine. For example, the fourth-century theologian Athanasius pointed out, the Psalms are "an epitome of the whole Scriptures." Basil, Bishop of Caesarea in the fourth century, noted that the Psalms were "a compendium of all theology." Martin Luther, the well-known Reformer of the sixteenth century, rightly called the Psalms "a little Bible, and the summary of the Old Testament." [2]

Reading the Psalms, we hear of God as Creator, Redeemer, Protector, Sustainer, Provider, Guide, and more. The most common way of speaking about God in the Psalms is through metaphor and simile. That's why we hear about God as our Shepherd, our King, our Warrior, our Mother, our Father, our Teacher, our Judge, and more.

learn more about these

ır relationship with Him as

ı opinion, the Psalms are a

ing into an art gallery with

and character on display.

complete by themselves,

ıses into the nature of God

ten Psalms for this book? I

earched Psalms in America

scovered is that millions of

ım God's Word. The results

ı uıaı scaıcıı aıc top ten list of Psalms in this series. But I took it one step further. I also searched for the deepest concerns that people have today. And what showed up were ten pressing needs that psychologists and researchers refer to as our fundamental human needs.

We have plenty of emotions floating around, but there are core emotions or fundamental human needs that people are continually looking to fulfill or have satisfied. It's why people keep searching, longing, and looking for something beyond themselves to find true meaning. It's like there's a giant hole in the center of our soul. Nothing can fill it and it shows up in the data, in the search.

What I found interesting was that when I laid out ten of the most common human fundamental needs, it corresponded to the top ten Psalms being searched for at the same time. To me, it spoke to how the Bible really understands us. It spoke to the divine inspiration of Scripture and how God has designed it to continually speak to the deepest part of the human experience. Not only to those in ancient times but also to each one of us today.

In terms of this message, the #1 searched Psalm in America over the past five years is Psalm 91. It's no secret why this Psalm is ranked #1. It's a Psalm that deals with the fundamental human concern of fear. Fear is a real emotion that can cause immense problems in our lives. Fear can immobilize you. It can make you sick. Fear can cause you to miss out on so much of what God has planned for your life.

There's not a person reading this who doesn't know how to relate to fear. We all know what it's like to be afraid, don't we? For me, there's nothing scarier than one of those rides that spin at the amusement park. If I see spinning teacups or some octopus ride flailing arms around and around, I'm heading in the other direction, ASAP! Now, you may laugh at that ☺, and you may not be able to connect with my fear of rides, but I'm pretty sure you can connect with my more substantial fears.

You may be surprised to hear this, but sometimes I'm afraid to stand in front of a group of people and give a speech. Sounds kind of weird for a guy who gives speeches for a living. But it's true. I'm afraid of the future for our kids. I look around me and I wonder how much further down the road of apostasy and secularism our country can go, and it concerns me. I'm afraid of seeing the life of someone I love get cut short. I'm afraid of getting some odd disease that is incurable. I've seen what cancer and other debilitating sicknesses can do and I don't like it. That, of course, leads to the ultimate question of what happens after we die. I can say I'm not afraid of what happens after I die, but the dying part of that equation, yeah, I'm not down for that part. I'd just as soon skip it.

In a world full of uncertainty, many of us wrestle with the unwelcome companion of fear. It's an intuitive dance we perform, an unspoken evaluation of our surroundings. No one instructs us to do this. It is how we are wired. We assess our fears which are the lurking threats to our peace. We do this against our hopes, the inspiration promising us security. Depending on which looks larger at the moment, we are either peaceful or in the depths of fear.

What is frustrating about fear is its incredible resilience. It can flourish in all conditions, through every season of life. When catastrophe strikes and our illusion of control crumbles, fear creeps in. Conversely, when we momentarily grasp the reins of our circumstances, we feel we can maintain control. Still, we wonder for how long? This is why the self-help section in bookstores is vast. We crave tools to grasp the world, yet peace remains elusive. A lasting escape from fear remains just out of reach for many.

That's why God gives us Psalm 91. It's a way you and I can say to fear, *"Hello Fear, It's Me and God."* Psalm 91 allows you and I to put fear on notice. The thing about Psalm 91 is that it will help you to properly size up your world. When you see your fear in light of who God is and what He does, you get a bigger perspective, and that's the most important thing to have when you're facing fear. Did you know that the phrase, fear not, or do not be afraid, appears 365 times in the Bible? That's once for every day of the year. God knew we would face this issue, so He loaded up the Bible with this command.

So, what is the solution when we are facing fear? According to Psalm 91, there are three things to overcome fears.

First, you can start by…

Enjoying the Protection of God

"¹He who dwells in the shelter of the Most High will abide in the shadow of the Almighty. ²I will say to the LORD, 'My refuge and my fortress, my God, in whom I trust.'" (Psalm 91:1-2)

The first thing you notice is that God is big in the opening two verses. In fact, the Bible uses four different phrases to describe God: The Most High, the Almighty, the LORD, and simply God. The psalmist is stating up front, that no matter what you're up against, because of God, you're going to be ok. He's saying, "Because of God, you're safe!"

But here's the thing, your safety isn't something that you can create. It's not something you can manufacture. You're safe because God is safe. God is big, and compared to Him, your situation is small. One of the ways you can overcome your fears is by comparing them to something bigger. In this case, it's comparing your fears to God.

When I was a kid, I remember running into a couple of bullies on the school playground when I was in the 1st grade. I didn't like those bullies because they were in 4th grade and were bigger than me, so naturally I was afraid. Whenever they came around, I'd high tail it out of there and head to another part of the playground. In other words, my fear caused me to miss out on the best parts of the playground. Until one day it dawned on me, I've got a resource available to me and I'm going to use it. I have a big brother in the 5th grade, and he's much bigger than those bullies. So, one day I stood my ground and said, "If you guys touch me, my brother's coming over and he's going to clobber you." They tested my theory until my brother noticed and came over to my defense. At that moment, the bigness of my brother triumphed over the bigness of my bullies. My fears sized up against my help, and my help was bigger. They never messed with me again.

That's the type of language the psalmist is using here. He's inspiring you to remember that God is bigger than any fear you might have. Real or not, God is bigger than all of it. Your fears may not be small, they may be big fears, and they may be real fears, but remember, God is greater!

Ultimately this issue of overcoming fears is about trust. Did you notice what it says at the end of verse two? It says, *"my God, in whom I trust."* This is similar to other Psalms that emphasize our trust in God.

"Some trust in chariots and some in horses, but we trust in the name of the LORD our God." (Psalm 20:7)

"As for God, His way is perfect; The Word of the LORD is tried; He is a shield unto all who trust in Him." (Ps 18:30 ERV)

"The LORD is my rock and my fortress and my deliverer; My

God, my strength, in whom I will trust; My shield and the horn of my salvation, my stronghold." (Psalm 18:2 NKJ)

"Show your marvelous lovingkindness by your right hand, O You who save those who trust in You from those who rise up against them." (Psalm 17:7 NKJ)

In all these passages we see a direct link between having freedom from fear and having trust in Almighty God.

Now, I want to teach you something interesting. I mentioned earlier that the phrase, *"Do not be afraid,"* is mentioned over 350 times in the Bible. And yet, what's also interesting is the Bible's first lesson in learning how to gain wisdom is to have fear.

But what kind of fear? That's the question. It is a fear of the Lord. In the book of Proverbs, we read, *"The fear of the Lord is the beginning of wisdom."* (Proverbs 9:10) How does this work?

If you were to sit down with these folks, these original readers of Psalms and Proverbs, and ask them, "Hey, teach me about wisdom or teach me about theology," do you know what they would say? They would say, "Sure, let's start with Fear God!"[5]

Let me show you something from the life of Jesus in Luke 12, *"[4]Dear friends, don't be afraid of those who want to kill your body; they cannot do any more to you after that. [5]But I'll tell you whom to fear. Fear God, who has the power to kill you and then throw you into hell. Yes, He's the one to fear. [6]What is the price of five sparrows—two copper coins? Yet God does not forget a single one of them. [7]And the very hairs on your head are all numbered. So don't be afraid; you are more valuable to God than a whole flock of sparrows."* (Luke 12:4-7)

What is Jesus saying here? Maybe you noticed the four-step sequence. Step one, don't be afraid of those who want to persecute you, they are small potatoes. Step two, fear God, He's a big deal. Step three, God cares about you. Step four, don't be afraid because you matter to God. You have value to God.

What is the point of this? Jesus is saying that if you want to be free from the fear of man, you're going to need a bigger fear. Listen friend, you won't be freed from fear by a self-help course. The way to find freedom is to find the one who can drive out those fears, and His name is Jesus.

We are learning here that God is not just powerful, but He is also personal. That's why the psalmist can say in verse two that God is *"my refuge, my fortress, and my God."*

There's another thing happening here that I don't want you to miss. You may have noticed that the psalmist describes the place, or location of safety. The verse starts by explaining that those who love God *"dwell in the shelter of the Most High."* Some translations say, *"secret place"* instead of *"shelter,"* and in many ways, this may be a better way to say it. In the original language, the word for "shelter" is סֵתֶר çêther, (say'-ther), and it means to be hidden or covered by something. It carries the idea of a hiding place. In biblical times, the *"secret place"* was a reference to the sanctuary, the temple, and this phrase would have been a metaphor for the original readers to understand.

Since the people of God did not live in the temple, the image of dwelling would signify remaining in the presence of God. It's a secret place because it is set apart from the world with all its chaos and danger. It is a secret place because it is made known to those who love God. This was as close as anyone could get to the presence of the Most High God.[6]

The result of dwelling in the secret place will be staying, or abiding, in the shadow of the Almighty. Did you catch that? The idea here is a comparison to the word protection and shade. Outside of the sanctuary, there is danger, but in the presence of God Almighty, there is safety. In the Ancient Near East, to be under the protection of a king is the same word used here for "shadow." To be under the *"shadow of the Almighty"* is to be under His protection and care.

The first way to overcome your fear is to enjoy the protection of God. How are you doing on that point?

Next, you can overcome your fear by…

Embracing the Promises of God

"[3]For He will deliver you from the snare of the fowler and from the deadly pestilence. [4]He will cover you with His pinions, and under His wings you will find refuge; His faithfulness is a shield and buckler. [5]You will not fear the terror of the night, nor the arrow that flies by day, [6]nor the pestilence that stalks in darkness, nor the destruction that wastes at noonday." (Ps 91:3)

Have you ever had a promise that was no good? Some of us from Gen X and older might remember those famous words from Bush 41, when he said, "Read my lips, no new taxes." It was intended to be a signature moment in his speech. And it was. The whole country remembered it. Yet, the poor guy was set up for failure from that point on. With the opposing party in control of congress, he had no choice but to make a deal that indeed raised taxes. He was hammered for it in the next election cycle and lost. Many political experts say the main reason for his political misfortune was his broken promise to the American people.

Life is like that; we make promises, we hold on to promises, and we break promises. Yet, one thing we learn early on is that a promise is only as good as the person giving it. Isn't that true? When it comes to God, the Bible reminds us, *"God is not a man, so He does not lie. He is not human, so He does not change His mind. Has He ever spoken and failed to act? Has He ever promised and not carried it through?"* (Numbers 23:19)

This verse reminds us that God is not like us. We may have a hard time living up to our promises, but God does not. Don't ever confuse your ability to carry out a promise with God's ability to carry out His promise. These are two different things. You are limited and finite, God is not. You are speculating about the future, God is not. You are trying to insert some type of control in a situation, but God is not...because He already has control of the whole show.

In this next portion of Psalm 91, there are three types of promises for those who love God.[7]

God's promises are versatile, individual, and miraculous. Let's first look at how versatile the promises of God are.

God's Promises are Versatile. In verses 3-6, we find analogies from snares and plagues to terrors, epidemics, and even flying arrows. The idea here is that God promises to protect His people in a way that covers a multitude of adversities. Things that surprise us, things that scare us, things that are sweeping, and things that are scheming. Almost every one of these situations comes at us like a flying arrow, deadly and without warning. And in that moment, we can freeze up with fear. And it can happen at any time, day or night.

In verses five and six, when it says night, day, darkness, and noon, the Bible is communicating that God is in protection mode 24/7. In other words, there isn't a time of day when God isn't on the clock watching over His people and upholding His promises.

Yet sandwiched in the middle of all these troubles is a beautiful promise, *"He will cover you with His feathers. He will shelter you with His wings. His faithful promises are your armor and protection."* (Psalm 91:4) I love this because it shows the tenderness of God alongside the defense of His people.

The Bible portrays God as both gentle and protective, like a bird shielding her chicks, as well as strong and fierce, like a warrior in armor. This is an important distinction because unfortunately, many people have a distorted understanding of God. Some view Him as solely judgmental, while others perceive Him as only merciful. The former belief was prevalent a few decades ago but persists in some circles today. The latter viewpoint, which I believe is more common in our culture today, sees God as endorsing personal choices due to His great love and mercy.

Some use this as a justification to do whatever they please, claiming it aligns with God's desire for their happiness. This is a mistake. We have to keep in mind that God is both tender and triumphant in perfect balance. As tender as God is to us, He is also triumphant over our enemies. Including the ones who attempt to deceive us and take us away from the plan and purpose of God in our lives.

God's Promises are Individual.

Next, we see that God's promises are individual. There are nine references to the word *"you"* or *"your"* in these four verses. It's as if God is saying to us, "Hey you!" The use of the word you is emphatic in this short passage. Meaning it is definite, forceful, absolute, and rich.

God is saying to those who love Him, to those who make, *"the Lord your dwelling place"* (v 9) that when great tragedy, judgment, evil, or curse come to the wicked, *"it will not come near you"* (v 7). The individual promise here is found in verse 8, *"You will only look with your eyes and see the recompense of the wicked."* The word recompense means reward. So, what we are learning here is that when God brings forth His judgment upon those who have rejected Him and have chosen to go their own way, the ones who have been sheltered by God will not be harmed. The judgment of God will pass over those who follow Jesus.

Some have mistakenly utilized this set of verses by placing them on a necklace, amulet, or charm. They do this hoping to keep evil spirits away or guarantee a victory on the battlefield, in the boxing ring, or in business. But that's not what the Bible is communicating here.

Psalm 91 talks about God's people being protected if they stay close to Him. In the New Testament, we learn that we are only protected by God if we trust in Jesus. He is the one who saves us from our biggest fears like death, hell, Satan, and God's punishment. Jesus did this by living a perfect life, dying for us, and coming back to life. When we believe in Him, we are safe forever. This is what the Christian gospel is all about.

If we don't have faith in Jesus, we don't have a safe place to go. This is why the phrase *"in Christ"* is important in the Bible. When we believe in Jesus, we become part of Him. We get all the good things that Jesus has, like His favor with the Father. As soon as we believe, Jesus becomes our safe place, our protection, and our Savior.

God's promises are Miraculous. We also learn that God's promises are miraculous. In verse 11, we read of an incredible promise about angels coming to the aid of those who walk with God, *"For He will command His angels concerning you to guard you in all your ways."* (Psalm 91:11) From this passage and others, we can safely say that one of the ways God protects His people is with angels. Check out Psalm 34 and Hebrews chapter one with me. *"The angel of the LORD encamps around those who fear Him and delivers them."* (Psalm 34:7) *"Therefore, angels are only servants—spirits sent to care for people who will inherit salvation."* (Hebrews 1:14)

This behind-the-scenes look in Psalm 34:7, and Hebrews 1:14 provides a glimpse into the cosmic battle between the forces of good and evil. We see this played out in other passages like 2

Kings 6. The story of when God opened the spiritual eyes of the servant to Elisha so that he could see the horses and chariots of fire standing ready to defend Elisha. The horses and chariots of fire are a callback and reminder of what God did for Elijah as he was ushered into God's presence four chapters earlier, in 2 Kings 2:11. The horses and chariots are representative of angelic squadrons sent on a special assignment.

We see a similar situation in Daniel 10 as an angel from God explains his spiritual battle lasting 21 days between him, Michael, and a demonic being called *"the prince of the kingdom of Persia."* (Daniel 10:13) Michael is important to our understanding here because Michael is the chief angel, and he is known as the warring angel and the one to battle on behalf of God's people. (Daniel 10:21, 12:1, Jude 9, Revelation 12:7) Lastly, on this point we gain a clear understanding of spiritual warfare from Paul's exhaustive list found in Ephesians 6.

Putting this all together, this multiplicity of passages lets us know that we are not alone as followers of Jesus. We have spiritual forces in Heaven fighting alongside us in the battle and it's miraculous.

So, we've learned another way to overcome our fears is to embrace the promises of God. Promises that are versatile, individual, and miraculous. What's the third and final way we can overcome our fears?

We can do so by…

Experiencing the Presence of God

"14The LORD says, 'I will rescue those who love Me. I will protect those who trust in My name. 15When they call on Me, I will answer; I will be with them in trouble. I will rescue and honor them. 16I will reward them with a long life and give them my salvation.'" (Psalm 91:14-16)

You might have noticed the shift in who's speaking in this final passage of Psalm 91. Bible commentators point out that Psalm 91 starts out with the psalmist writing about his experience in the first person in verses 1-2. Then in verses 3-13, the tone shifts from first person to second and third person…like a teacher telling the people of God what to expect. And here, in the final part, verses 14-16, the tone shifts to, "The LORD says." Here we have the voice of a prophet declaring to the people of God the voice of God concerning this topic.

According to this final set of verses, the one who loves God, the one who calls on God, can count on seven things. Here they are: God will rescue them, protect them, answer them, be with them, honor them, reward them with a long life, and provide salvation.

Here's the thing, when you call on God, when you trust in His name, when you love Jesus, He doesn't just put up with you. He doesn't just tolerate you. We do that with people, don't we? But Jesus doesn't do that with us. I don't have time to go into all seven of these truths, but the bottom line to all of this is God brings us close to Himself and allows us to experience His presence. And when we are in His presence, our fear of those things that have been chasing us down simply vanishes. Another way to say it is the brightness of His presence floods our life and no darkness can be found. You see, God doesn't tolerate us, He transforms us. And He does it through our being in His presence.

Think of it this way, when you get to Heaven one day, do you think you will have any fears standing in the presence of God? Will you have any worries? Will you be afraid, scared, terrified, or anxious? You don't need to be. Let me share with you why.

In the New Testament, John writes, "*13And God has given us His Spirit as proof that we live in Him and He in us. 14Furthermore, we have seen with our own eyes and now testify that the Father sent His Son to be the Savior of the world. 15All who declare that Jesus is the Son of God have God living in them, and they live in God...17So we will not be afraid on the day of judgment, but we can face Him with confidence because we live like Jesus here in this world. 18Such love has no fear, because perfect love expels all fear. If we are afraid, it is for fear of punishment, and this shows that we have not fully experienced His perfect love*". (1 John 4:13-18)

I don't know where you stand spiritually today. You might be super close to God, like Jesus' little brother. Or you might be a million miles away from God. It doesn't matter because no matter where you are, you matter to God. If you're not close. Jesus is inviting you to come closer. What's holding you back? Is it fear? Is it guilt? Is it disappointment? Listen, all of those things will do nothing but keep you away from the very peace, safety, security, and joy of God. I want to encourage you today to press into God's presence and don't let fear keep you away from what God has for you.

My father passed away in 2008. About five years earlier, the doctors discovered he had cancer. They treated it. It went away and he was cancer-free. But eventually it came back. He began to experience discomfort, but he ignored it. He kept putting it off because he didn't want to hear he had cancer again. He was afraid to hear those words. So, in an effort to avoid his fears, he ignored what he needed to do.

Eventually the pain became unbearable, and he went back in. But it was too late. By then the cancer had spread into areas where there was nothing the doctors or treatment could do. My dad was the life of the party, he had many great years ahead of him, but he let his fear get the best of him. He let his fear steal away years of joy.

Now, my dad was a Christian. He is in Heaven. He trusted Jesus as his personal Lord and Savior. I will see him again and when I do, he will probably ask me why I put him in the sermon. The point is not to let the joys of life be stolen by your fears.

Don't be afraid to face your fears. One of the best ways to do that is to get into God's presence.

How do you do that, you might ask. By doing four things. Get in the Bible. Get into worship. Get into prayer. Get with people.

Get in the Word. *"The Word of the Lord endures forever. And this is the Word that was proclaimed to you"* (1 Peter 1:25 NET)

Start your day out with 5 to 15 minutes of Bible reading. If you don't like reading, you can have it read to you through a Bible

App. This is one of the ways you connect with God every day. We need this because we are tapping into His Word that endures forever. Long after the fears we are facing today have faded away, God's Word will still be here. His Word will still be directing, guiding, and declaring truth to us and the generations to follow. I encourage you to tap into God's source of everlasting truth.

Get into Worship. *"Worship the LORD with gladness. Come before Him, singing with joy."* (Psalm 100:2)

Sing, contemplate, meditate, or reflect on God through music and song. It's a powerful way to experience God's presence. Worship has a unique way of displacing fears, worries, and anxiety. It really does. Many times I have turned up the music and sung to God even when I didn't feel like it. Don't underestimate the power of worship through music.

Get into Prayer. *"⁶Don't worry about anything; instead, pray about everything. Tell God what you need and thank Him for all He has done. ⁷Then you will experience God's peace, which exceeds anything we can understand. His peace will guard your hearts and minds as you live in Christ Jesus."* (Phil 4:6-7)

The way to experience God's peace is through prayer. Did you notice that you not only experience God's peace when you pray but His peace then acts like a guard, like a soldier that doesn't allow fear to come back into your heart and mind? Prayer is powerful.

Get with some People. *"²⁴We should keep on encouraging each other to be thoughtful and to do helpful things. ²⁵Some people have given up the habit of meeting for worship, but we must not* *do that. We should keep on encouraging each other, especially since you know that the day of the Lord's coming is getting closer."* (Hebrews 10:24-25 CEV)

This last point is so important. Christians are like charcoal; we burn brightest and hottest when we're closer together. When we separate and go solo, we lose our effectiveness. It's important to be part of a weekly worship service. It's important to be a part of a Life Group. Why? Because these are the people you end up doing life with. No one can go through life alone and we should not have to. As Christians, we are here for each other. A group of fellow believers will pray with you, support you, serve with you, grow with you, and build a long-lasting connection to you, your family, and the family of God. I can't encourage you enough to get into a small group.

So, what have we learned so far? We discovered that we could overcome our fear by…

- Enjoying the Protection of God (v 1-2)

  - Embracing the Promises of God (v 3-13)

  - Experiencing the Presence of God (v 14-16)

Through this journey of Psalm 91 we came to see the assurance of safety and security in times of fear come from a wholehearted trust in the presence of the LORD who has entrusted those who love Him to His angels for protection and deliverance.[8]

But there's one final story I'd like to share with you. In early August of this year, we all watched with sadness as the deadliest wildfire in the US in over 100 years broke out on the Hawaiian island of Maui. As the scope of this human tragedy sunk in, over 115 lives were lost in Lahaina and hundreds were missing. Twenty-seven hundred homes were destroyed in the fire as the flames, heat and embers swept across the island. Nothing was left. Almost nothing.

In a neighborhood reduced to ash, in contrast to barren and desolate remains, stands a 100-year-old red-roofed house.

Owner Dora Atwater Millikin put the survival of the home down to a handful of routine changes during a recent renovation — none of which were aimed at surviving such a disaster.

One decision that helped the house survive the wildfire was replacing the asphalt roof with one made out of heavy-gauge metal. The house may also have benefited from not being too close to neighboring properties — often the main fuel for fires — instead being bordered on three sides by the ocean, a road, and an empty lot.

They also unknowingly improved the property's odds of survival, having lined the ground with stones up to the drip line of the roof, and cut down foliage that was up against the outside walls. They told the Los Angeles Times, "We love old buildings, so we just wanted to honor the heritage of the building," said Millikin. "And we didn't change the building in any way — we just restored it."

Psalm 91:1 says, *"Whoever dwells in the shelter of the Most High will rest in the shadow of the Almighty."* God isn't merely providing a "refuge," a place of rest… Or a "fortress," a place of defense. It says that the Lord IS these things.

You see, Psalm 91 is written to dwellers. It promises deliverance and protection not to everyone, but to dwellers, those who maintain their walk with Him. Those who love Jesus and long for Him and not just the benefits He provides.

The house with the red roof didn't avoid the fires, it survived them. It was marked, but it survived. God promises to keep us as we dwell in Him. He is the refuge, and His love for us is the guarantee that even though the fire purifies us, it will not destroy us, and if we remain in Him, we will stand.

Chapter 2

Cultivating a Quiet Heart in a Loud World

Psalm 23

In his new book, *The 16 Undeniable Laws of Communication*, John Maxwell tells a story about English actor Charles Laughton. He was famous for his readings of poetry and other literary passages. Laughton was attending a Christmas party with a large family in London. Well into the evening, the host decided that each person in attendance should read or recite a favorite passage, one that reminded them most of the Spirit of Christmas. Laughton's turn came near the end, and he recited, in his beautifully trained voice, the Twenty-Third Psalm. Everyone applauded his effort, and the process continued. Within minutes, all had participated except one elderly aunt, who had dozed off in a corner of the room. She was especially loved, and they gently woke her, explained what was going on, and asked her to take part. She thought for a moment, and then began in her shaky voice, *"The Lord is my Shepard, I shall not want..."* The room hushed as she continued, and when she finished, tears were dripping down every face. Upon leaving, one of the younger members of the family thanked Laughton for coming and commented about the difference in the response of the family to the two "readings." In one case, appreciation; in the other, deep connection and involvement. "How do you account for it?" asked the young man. Shaking his head, Laughton looked at him and replied simply, "I know the Psalm ... she knows the shepherd."[9]

There's something to knowing the Shepherd of Psalm 23. Some know of him from a distance. Some know of him by name only. Some know of him through childhood stories. Others know him through a lifetime of experience. The question for you and me today is, do you only know of the Psalm of the shepherd, or do you know the shepherd of the Psalm?

What does God's Word have to say about this?

"Cast all your anxiety on Him, because He cares for you." (1 Peter 5:7 BSB)

"When my anxious thoughts multiply within me, your comforts delight me." (Psalm 94:19 BSB)

"Do not be anxious about anything. Instead, in every situation, through prayer and petition with thanksgiving, tell your requests to God. And the peace of God that surpasses all understanding will guard your hearts and minds in Christ Jesus." (Philippians 4:6-7 NET)

Now when applying the truths of the Bible to our lives, it's important to remember that God's truth always triumphs over our fears. His awareness strikes down our anxieties. God's wisdom replaces our worry. And God's stability overcomes our stress.

This is an important issue in our time. According to a recent article in Psychology Today, "Anxiety disorder affects some 40 million adult Americans. And for every person with a diagnosed disorder, there are many more who struggle with anxiety symptoms: sleep problems, worries that won't cease, fear and uneasiness, or shortness of breath."

As bad as the rate of anxiety disorders is among adults, its prevalence among children is even more worrisome: 38% of girls between the ages of 13 and 17, and 26% of boys have an anxiety disorder, according to the National Institutes of Mental Health. Additionally, anxiety is the most common mental health concern on college campuses today. With anxiety so widespread, is it any wonder that we're seeing college students who demand "safe spaces," and" trigger warnings?"[10]

Anxiety is a big problem that affects not just our mental health but our culture as a whole. Our way of life encourages anxiety and its negative effects. Anxiety makes us scared and easily irritated, which can lead to anger. When we're scared or angry, we don't think clearly or calmly. We're more likely to react impulsively.

It doesn't help us that the news, social media, and politicians all contribute to our anxiety by constantly telling us to be afraid. They use dramatic language and scary stories to get our attention. This makes our anxiety levels stay high all the time. In fact, a recent Rasmussen survey found that 76% of Americans are afraid of political violence. It's difficult to find peace in a world that's so loud.

Experts tell us that the sound of a rocket launch is one of the loudest sounds you'll ever hear. A shotgun and fighter jet aren't too far behind. But human experience outweighs the experts, because we all know that the loudest sound of all is the sound of an anxious soul.

When your soul is anxious you can't find peace. When your heart is anxious you can't find rest. When your mind is anxious you can't find a sense of quietness or calm.

So, the big question for us today is how do we overcome our anxiousness and Cultivate a Quiet Heart in a Loud World?

Thankfully, God Gives us a Solution.

In Psalm 23, we discover that God is a source of profound comfort. It assures us that Jesus is our caring Shepherd, guiding and guarding us through life's wild journey. Psalm 23 defeats anxiety by painting a vivid picture of God's loving provision, comparing us to sheep under His watchful eye.

Amidst green pastures and beside tranquil waters, God replenishes our souls. Even in the shadows of the trials of life, His presence brings assurance and courage. His guidance and protection offer security. Knowing His goodness and mercy calms our anxious hearts. Ultimately, Psalm 23 promises an eternal home in God's presence, erasing anxiety with the hope of lasting peace.

In this famous Psalm, we discover four truths that help us to overcome our anxiety.

First, we overcome our anxiety by …

Knowing the Shepherd

"¹The LORD is my Shepherd; I shall not want. ²He makes me lie down in green pastures. He leads me beside still waters. ³He restores my soul. He leads me in paths of righteousness for His name's sake." (Psalm 23:1-3)

In real life shepherding, sheep are known to recognize and respond to the voice of their shepherd. This behavior is well-documented in agricultural and pastoral settings. Shepherds develop a close bond with their sheep through daily interaction, and the sheep become familiar with the unique sound and tone of their shepherd's voice.

When the shepherd calls or speaks to the sheep, they often become attentive, gather around, or follow in the direction the shepherd is leading. This strong recognition of the shepherd's voice is a result of the trust and relationship that develops between the shepherd and the flock over time. It's a beautiful illustration used in Psalm 23 to symbolize the close relationship between God and His people.

The idea of Jesus being the Shepherd of His people is not exclusive to Psalm 23. In other passages the Bible clearly teaches us this same truth.

"Oh, save your people and bless your heritage! Be their shepherd and carry them forever." (Psalm 28:9)

"O Shepherd of Israel, pay attention, you who lead Joseph like a flock of sheep!" (Psalm 80:1 NET)

The prophet Isaiah predicted the coming Messiah would be like a shepherd, *"He will feed His flock like a shepherd. He will carry the lambs in His arms, holding them close to His heart. He will gently lead the mother sheep with their young."* (Isa 40:11)

Jesus identified Himself as the expected Good Shepherd, *"I am the Good Shepherd. I know my sheep and my sheep know Me."* (John 10:14)

Hebrews refers to Jesus as the Great Shepherd, *"Now may the God of peace, who through the blood of the eternal covenant brought back from the dead our Lord Jesus, that Great Shepherd of the sheep, equip you with every good thing to do His will."* (Hebrews 13:20-21 BSB)

Finally, Peter, one of Jesus' closest disciples, refers to Him as the Chief Shepherd who will return again for His sheep, *"And when the Chief Shepherd appears, you will receive the crown of glory that will never fade away."* (1 Peter 5:4 BSB)

All of this together indicates to us that God desires to know us and for us to know Him. Other passages in the Bible mention that God desires for us to be His friend. Did you know that? Some people find this surprising. Especially if you grew up in a very strict or liturgical type of Christian experience. In those settings God is revered (and should be), but sometimes in a way in which people think God is far off and wants to keep it that way. But that's not true. We are learning through Psalm 23 that God wants to be our Shepherd. He wants to be close to us.

One of my favorite Bible teachers, Timothy Keller, taught on this subject by referring to Psalm 25:14, *"The friendship of the LORD is for those who fear Him, and He makes known to them His covenant."*

Job reminds us of his connection, *"God's friendship was felt in my home."* (Job 29:4)

James, the half-brother of Jesus, writes, *"Abraham believed God, and God counted him as righteous because of his faith. He was even called the friend of God."* (James 2:23)

Keller goes on to say, "Friendship with God is an infinite friendship in which God confides in us. It's possible because God makes it possible." He draws this conclusion based on the original language used in Psalm 25 and through a direct inference of the divine nature of a triune God. One God in three persons. In other words, because of the trinity, God was in relationship long before He created us, so relationship is a part of God's divine nature. This is important because if God wasn't one God in three persons, He would be all power with no love. But because love is forged in and through relationships and God is love, we know and experience God as all power and all love.

Keller continues by noting that this contrasts with our culture which emphasizes spirituality in a loose sense. Meaning when people say, "I'm spiritual but not religious" what they mean is "I want to feel as though I'm connected to something divine, but I want to live my life the way that I want to live. I don't want the discipline or discipleship that goes with a biblical example of following Jesus."[11]

As a Christian you have a direct line, a direct connection to God. Through Christ, you have been made a friend of God. You don't have to go to someone else to gain access to Jesus. You can go directly to Him and He will transform your life.

You don't have to wait for someone to bring news from Jesus

to you. You already have access once you've invited Him into your life. You have that connection. It's real, it's relevant, and it's relational. Before the time of Jesus people didn't have this type of connection. God dwelt in the Holy of Holies, in the Temple. But now, because of what Jesus did upon the cross, you have access to God's presence in your life. Let me explain it this way.

Pastor Thomas Selby (1846-1910) who lived during the second half of the 1800s and into the early 1900s, tells the story of a lady who made a living by bringing the correct time from Greenwich, England to jewelry shops in small towns near London. She had a special clock that her father had passed down to her, and she would get it regulated by the authorities at the Greenwich Observatory. Every Friday she would go there to get the correct time and then bring it to her clients who paid her a small fee for this service. This lady was a part of an older time when people had to rely on others to bring them the correct time. Nowadays, many towns and businesses are directly connected to Greenwich and can get the correct time every day.[12]

Even more, one hundred and twenty years later, no one relies on someone bringing them a correct clock because we're all connected to synchronized clocks through our cell phone providers. Our digital clocks are connected via satellite and WIFI to International Atomic Time, a high-precision time standard kept by over 450 atomic clocks in over 80 national laboratories worldwide.[13] Today we have instant access to the correct time in real-time all the time.

In the past people who wanted to learn about God had to rely on prophets and priests to bring them a message from God. But now, through Jesus, people have an uninterrupted connection with God, and we gain direct wisdom because we are continuously connected through the Holy Spirit and the written Word of God. We have become a friend of God and are connected to Him in real-time all the time.

Verse one solidifies the fact that we are connected to Jesus because He is our shepherd. Verses two and three go on to tell us that God does three specific things to help us deal with our anxiety.

He Provides Spiritual Nourishment. *"He makes me lie down in green pastures."* (v 2)

How many of you know that when you eat healthy you feel better? When you eat poorly, you feel horrible. The same thing is true in your spiritual life. When you partake of healthy spiritual food your spirit feels better. You'll develop a more non-anxious spirit the more you eat healthy spiritual food. As parents, we all know this truth, don't we? As a good parent, you only provide the best food for your kids. Why? Because they are counting on you to survive.

That same thing is true for your spiritual life. This verse shows us that Jesus leads His followers to partake of good spiritual food. When you follow Jesus you'll never lack positive spiritual nourishment. The Bible says that God also provides under shepherds for His people, and they are expected to feed the flock. (Acts 20:28, 1 Peter 5:2, John 21:15-17) We also learn from other passages that our food for the soul is the Word of God. (Hebrews 5:12-14, 1 Peter 2:2)

He Provides Spiritual Restoration. *"He leads me beside still waters."* (v 2)

Next, we see this vivid picture representing a place of rest and restoration. As a shepherd leads his sheep to peaceful waters for rest and cleansing, so Jesus also restores or refreshes the soul. Jesus provides forgiveness and peace for those who follow Him. The prophet Isaiah mentions that God will guide His people to a place of rest, *"They will neither hunger nor thirst. The searing sun will not reach them anymore. For the LORD in His mercy will lead them; He will lead them beside cool waters."* (Isaiah 49:10) It's interesting to note that the sheep are not being taken to a rushing stream or raging water, but rather to a still, calming lagoon. In the original language, there's an emphasis on the kind or type of water that we are being led to.

In the Old Testament, turbulent waters speak of distress (Isaiah 43:2, 2 Samuel 5:20), but calm waters speak of spiritual cleansing, and with that come calm and peace. (Leviticus 11:32, 16:4, Numbers 19:7, and Exodus 30:18) If your life is turbulent, check around you to see what kind of stream you're drinking from? What kind of water are you bringing into your life? If your friends are toxic, your life might be toxic too. If your personal connections are confused, there's a good chance you will be. If your surroundings are disorderly, your spirit may be disordered as well.

If you're filled with anxiousness, you need to seek out the places where you can find calm waters provided to you by Jesus. Worship, the word, prayer, meditation, long walks of contemplation as you review God's word along the way and

44

listen to calming worship. These are the still waters God has set up for you. In the stillness, in the calm, in the quietness, you will find restoration, *"³He restores my soul."* Restore means a return to the original state.

Just like regular sheep that tend to stray from the shepherd's presence, we tend to do the same. But God never leaves us nor forsakes us, Jesus is on a constant and never-ending mission to bring us back and restore us. He is making and molding us into the people He wants us to be. In fact, if you've strayed away from the fold, He's calling you back home today.

"³So Jesus told them this story: ⁴If a man has a hundred sheep and one of them gets lost, what will he do? Won't he leave the ninety-nine others in the wilderness and go to search for the one that is lost until he finds it? ⁵And when he has found it, he will joyfully carry it home on his shoulders. ⁶When he arrives, he will call together his friends and neighbors, saying, 'Rejoice with me because I have found my lost sheep.' ⁷In the same way, there is more joy in heaven over one lost sinner who repents and returns to God than over ninety-nine others who are righteous and haven't strayed away." (Luke 15:3-7)

He Provides Spiritual Guidance. *"He leads me in paths of righteousness."* (v 3)

If you wanted to climb the highest mountain peak in the world, you wouldn't attempt to do it alone. You would hire a guide. Someone who's been to the summit and knows how to guide you to the top. The same thing happens in our walk with Jesus. He came to our planet and took upon Himself our human nature, in tandem with His divine nature, so that He could show

45

us the way home. He is the guide you need to navigate through the situations you face. You may be facing a tough situation today and you don't know the right way. It is creating turbulence in your heart and anxiousness in your soul. The Bible tells us that Jesus is the one who will lead you down the right path.

This word path, in this text, means "wagon tracks." A shepherd knows how to look for the wagon tracks to lead his sheep home. These are the right tracks. These tracks are the paths of rightness or righteousness. The wrong tracks, like the track of an animal or a band of robbers, are paths that lead you astray and into danger. These paths complicate your anxiety. These paths lead you to continued confusion and feelings of lostness, fear, and panic.

There's a double meaning here. Not only will God lead you on the right path, but it also means that God will never lead you down a path of unrighteousness. Jesus always leads us in the right way, which is the way home. This is one of the ways you can find out if your actions, attitudes, or behavior are on the right path. Is it a path Jesus would take you on? If not, then stay off that path.

This is why you really need to know your Bible and how to best understand it. There are numerous misinterpretations of God's word floating around on almost every topic imaginable today. Misapplication of God's word is leading many people astray.

So, here's what I can teach you today.

First, remember that Scripture will always interpret Scripture.

Second, never build an entire doctrine on one passage.

Third, a literal historical-grammatical approach secures the original message.

Ask three questions when interpreting the Bible (in this order):

- What does it say?

- What does it mean? (to the original audience)

- What does it mean to me today?

We are faced with a plethora of decisions today. Lifestyle choices, political animosity, fractured allegiances, feigned compassion, and talking heads galore fill the airways and profiles of every media channel. It's difficult and challenging to know who is telling the truth. Always remember, truth is a person, not a proposition, and that person is Jesus.

So, the first way to overcome your anxiousness is to know the Shepherd.

Next, you can overcome your anxiousness by…

Embracing the Valley

"Even though I walk through the valley of the shadow of death, I will fear no evil, for you are with me; your rod and your staff, they comfort me." (Psalm 23:4)

Have you ever been in a dark situation? Have you ever had to walk through a time in your life that was gloomy, obscure, or dangerous? Some of you are walking through a season like that today. The question becomes what do you do when you are faced with a valley in life? And we're not talking about soft and gentle valleys, we're talking about valleys of darkness and looming death.

Helping us to understand the original context, one commentator writes, "The hill country of Judah is broken up by narrow and steep ravines difficult to descend and ascend, dark, gloomy, and abounding in caves, the home of wild beasts and robbers."[14]

When you walk through a valley like this it's difficult to stay hopeful. Death and darkness seem to abound. The death and darkness spoken of here are not limited to the physical, they may be relational, they may be connected to God's plan for your life that you think is over, or your business and career. In either of these cases, things don't look good and hope for life and light in your situation is all but gone. Despair breeds anxiety and in those moments of life we look for hope. We cry out for help.

Psalm 23 teaches us that even though you may be going through a situation that is dangerous, damaging, or deadly, God will be with you. Jesus is your shepherd, and He will be right beside you. The Bible reminds us, *"I will fear no evil, for you are with me."*

Did you notice how the passage changed from referring to the shepherd as *"He"* in (v 1-3) to *"you"* in (v 4)? At the point of danger in your life God becomes more personal, doesn't He? In the first three verses the picture is one of the shepherd leading us from the front. But here in verse four we sense the shepherd walking alongside us and protecting us as his sheep.

Knowing that Jesus is alongside us in the valley helps us to overcome the anxiety of isolation. Especially when that isolation happens in dark times, which is often the way it happens. Companionship is good when you're pressed in on all sides, but divine protection is even better. We learn that our Shepherd is armed with His rod and staff, *"your rod and your staff, they comfort me."* The rod was used to beat away the enemies of the sheep and the staff was used to keep the sheep in line. God knows we need both as followers of Jesus. We need His continual protection from our enemies, and we need His discipline to keep in line.

The phrase *"You are with me"* has a deeper meaning. It signifies that God is here to protect and provide for you. This is a significant theme in the Bible, which was first introduced by God to Jacob in Bethel when God said, *"I will be with you."* (Genesis 28:15) Likewise, God told Moses *"I am with you."* (Exodus 3:12) It found full expression in the prophecy of Immanuel, *"God is with us."* (Isaiah 7:14) And finally, in the New Testament, Jesus promised to be with us always, till the end of the age. (Matthew 28:20)

One of Jesus' original apostles, a man named Paul, had a remarkable understanding of this point. One could easily say that Paul lived out the very essence of this small but impactful verse. In one of his letters to the early believers in the city of Corinth, he walks them through this idea of finding God's strength in times of weakness. It's the same idea as the valley of darkness described in Psalm 23.

The question becomes, how do you maintain cool assurance under pressure?

After explaining to the Corinthians, the complexities of his valley, Paul shares how he overcomes the anxiety of dark times by relying on God's strength. *"⁷I was given a thorn in my flesh, a messenger from Satan to torment me and keep me from becoming proud. ⁸Three different times I begged the Lord to take it away. ⁹Each time He said, 'My grace is all you need. My power works best in weakness.' So now I am glad to boast about my weaknesses, so that the power of Christ can work through me. ¹⁰That's why I take pleasure in my weaknesses, and in the insults, hardships, persecutions, and troubles that I suffer for Christ. For when I am weak, then I am strong."* (2 Cor 12:7-10)

One of the ways to overcome the anxiety of a tough situation is to embrace what God is allowing you to go through. Paul clearly says the dark times do not distract him. He actually says he embraces the valley because through the valley God's strength is shown. Insults, hardships, persecutions, and troubles, none of it moved Paul away from his shepherd. He embraced the situation and trusted in Christ to bring him through it.

How are you doing in this area? I'm sure we all can use a little more encouragement to emulate the life of Paul. One of the best illustrations I attempt to keep in mind when I'm going through a valley of darkness is to remember the darkroom of God's development. For those of us who remember old-school photography, you may recall the dark room. After the picture was taken the film was removed from the camera, washed in chemicals, and slowly and meticulously developed in the dark room. When the picture was fully developed, it was ready to come out and be put on display for the world to see.

Friend, God may very well have you in the darkroom today. But don't be anxious, He is developing you. He is processing your gifts. He is washing the chemicals off your life and in the process, He is creating a beautiful picture for you and others to enjoy.

Pastor Skip Heitzig of Calvary Chapel in Albuquerque, New Mexico, says it this way, "God uses the darkroom to turn your negatives into positives."

Don't let the valley of darkness scare you. Embrace the darkroom of God's development and be patient as you go through His process of refinement.

You can overcome anxiety by knowing the Shepherd and embracing the valley. According to Psalm 23, what's a third way to overcome your anxiety?

We can do so by...

Ignoring Our Enemies.

"You prepare a table before me in the presence of my enemies; You anoint my head with oil; my cup overflows." (Psalm 23:5)

One of the quickest ways to raise the level of anxiety in your life is to be in a high-pressure situation. Maybe it's a critical job interview. You've made it past the prelims and you're on the final list of highly qualified candidates. You're invited in and all you can think of is, "Don't mess this up."

Maybe you're an athlete and you're called on to kick the winning goal at the World Cup. As you line up to kick the final penalty shot all you can think of is, "Don't miss this."

Maybe you're about to meet your future in-laws and you've been warned by your girlfriend how critical it is to make a good first impression and all you can think of is, "Don't be an idiot."

In all these cases, your heart races and your breathing quickens as the anxiety of the moment builds. Pressure at work, in athletics, or when dating is one thing, but being in a high-pressure situation with your enemies intensifies the anxiety to a level that for some can be unbearable. Have you been there before?

When you read this passage, it's easy to conclude that David is surrounded by his enemies. At first glance it appears that this encounter with his enemies will be a tense and anxious situation, especially because his enemy has the upper hand. But is David's tent surrounded by those who want to destroy him?

In scripture our enemies are never to be taken lightly. If David's tent is being encircled by enemies, it would seem untimely to throw a celebratory banquet. However, it is likely that the mention of a celebration is actually an anticipation of a celebration of victory over his enemies. This celebration then would involve the enemies being present in a banquet hall as captives, or, as some commentators conclude, some type of treaty with his defeated rivals.

Did you notice the change of scenery between verses four and five? Once David declares, *"You are with me"* in verse 4, the remainder of Psalm 23 changes. It moves from anxiousness to confidence. David is comforted, he is at a banquet, he enjoys the favor of God, and he will spend eternity with the Lord in verse 6.

What's going on here?

Let's go back to the high-pressure situations from before. What if you already knew you had the job, how do you think the interview would go? What if you already knew you were going to make the goal? What if you already met your future in-laws before the big meeting, and you and your future father-in-law already worked out how the meeting would go? In all these examples your anxiety would be diminished because you already knew the outcome.

When you already know the outcome, your tension lowers. Now, you may not know the outcome of most of the situations you face, but you can know the One who does.

We spend way too much time worrying about what our enemies think about us. In reality, it doesn't matter what they think. What matters is what God thinks. What matters is that nothing can keep us from the love of God that is found in Jesus. Paul reminds us of this great truth in Romans 8,

"31 What then shall we say to these things? If God is for us, who is against us? 32 He who did not spare His own Son, but delivered Him over for us all, how will He not also with Him freely give us all things? 33 Who will bring a charge against God's elect? God is the one who justifies; 34 who is the one who condemns? Christ Jesus is He who died, yes, rather who was raised, who is at the right hand of God, who also intercedes for us. 35 Who will separate us from the love of Christ? Will tribulation or distress, or persecution, or famine, or nakedness, or peril, or sword?

36 Just as it is written 'FOR YOUR SAKE WE ARE BEING

PUT TO DEATH ALL DAY LONG; WE WERE CONSIDERED AS SHEEP TO BE SLAUGHTERED.' [37]But in all these things we overwhelmingly conquer through Him who loved us. [38]For I am convinced that neither death, nor life, nor angels, nor principalities, nor things present, nor things to come, nor powers, [39]nor height, nor depth, nor any other created thing, will be able to separate us from the love of God, which is in Christ Jesus our Lord." (Romans 8:31-39 NASB)

When David declares that God is preparing a table, anointing his head with oil, and filling his cup to overflowing this is what he's saying…nothing will stop God from moving in your life.

In Romans 8, Paul puts believers in a courtroom and then brings us through the progression by asking, Who is against us, who will bring a charge, who condemns, who will separate us?

He then brings forth a set of witnesses attempting to prosecute us by asking, *"…will tribulation, or distress, or persecution, or famine, or nakedness, or peril, or sword?"*

He then concludes to the judge and jury, …in all these things we overwhelmingly conquer through Him who loved us.

When you understand how secure you are in God's love then it doesn't matter what your enemies think, feel, or do.

- If God delivers you, you're anchored in His love.

- If God allows persecution, you're anchored in His love.

- If God provides, you're anchored in His love.

- If God delays, you're anchored in His love.

David knew this, Paul knew this, and countless believers

throughout the pages of scripture have all known the strength and freedom of this powerful truth. Since the pages of the Bible and throughout the pages of history, millions of additional followers of Jesus have experienced this truth as well. Even during our day, millions upon millions of followers of Jesus are waking up to this truth as our world continues to get darker and darker and the enemies of God attempt to knock us off course. But they will not be able to win as we stand firm in the truth of God's word and the strength of our convictions that God will indeed prepare a table for me in the presence of my enemies. He will deliver me. He will protect me. He will provide for me according to His will and plan.

When you have this type of conviction, this type of confidence, anxiety has no home in your soul.

You can overcome anxiety by knowing the Shepherd, embracing the valley, and ignoring your enemies. According to Psalm 23, what's the final way to overcome your anxiety?

It's by…

Focusing on My Future.

"Surely goodness and mercy shall follow me all the days of my life, and I shall dwell in the house of the LORD forever." (Psalm 23:6)

One of the things we did when our kids were younger was pray with them Psalm 23 at bedtime. At the conclusion of one of those prayer times, Carson, 3 years old at the time, asked his mom, "Mom, who are Shirley and Goodness? And why are they following me everywhere I go?" It was a great moment.

55

This last verse is an amazing promise to those who follow Jesus. It promises God's special presence both now and forever. Sometimes, when we are the most tangled up inside, the most anxious and stressed out, it's beneficial to simply stop, slow down, and focus on God's future for us while we're in the present.

What are God's promises? What is Heaven going to be like? This type of forward-thinking and divine planning moves you out of the current situation and into a better place.

Without godly wisdom, some may say that looking into the future will exacerbate your feelings of anxiety. What the Bible is getting at here is to recognize your current situation, be mindful of it, and be real, but remember that God gives us the promise of Heaven for a reason.

Staying in the present is referred to as practicing mindfulness. One researcher writes, "Practicing mindfulness can be an effective way to manage feelings of stress and anxiety and can even be used as a relaxation technique for panic disorder.[15] This meditation technique can help you slow down racing thoughts, decrease negativity, and calm both your mind and body."[16] This is a good practice. But as a follower of Jesus, as you slow down, reflect, and renew your mind remember how God's promises meet you in the present. Medical professionals today are learning what many Christians have known for years. When we focus our minds on the things of God the tension and stress of life are reduced.

There are two truths I want you to see here. This first phrase, *"goodness and mercy shall follow me all the days of my* *life"* is a far deeper concept than having two unknown attributes floating around the ether of our existence as we go about our days. What this phrase really means is to have "God's good loyal love" in abundant supply because He never forsakes His covenant with us.

God's love for you is a faithful covenant love. The most amazing aspect of God's love is His commitment to love us in spite of our unfaithfulness. His covenant to love is based upon His character and His promise, *"He always stands by His covenant — the commitment He made to a thousand generations."* (Psalm 105:8) God's love has never been conditioned on us, or our actions (good or bad).

Some translations say, *"Surely your goodness and unfailing love will pursue me all the days of my life."* The word pursue is a great way to say it. In other words, there is nothing you can do to get God to stop loving you. Do you remember back to Romans 8? What was it that could prevent us from receiving God's love? Do you recall?

Here it is again, *"[38] For I am convinced that neither death, nor life, nor angels, nor principalities, nor things present, nor things to come, nor powers, [39] nor height, nor depth, nor any other created thing, will be able to separate us from the love of God, which is in Christ Jesus our Lord."* (Romans 8:38-39 NASB)

So, I ask you again, what is it that can separate you from the love of God, in Christ Jesus? The answer, of course, is nothing.

The second truth concerns Heaven. David concludes Psalm 23 by declaring, *"I shall dwell in the house of the LORD forever."* This is an obvious declaration that because of God's protection and loving pursuit, David understood that he would be in the presence of God forever. In the original language, "forever" technically means, "for the length of days," and was a reference to David's hope of being with the Lord all the days of his life.

We know from studying the Bible that much of our understanding of what happens to us in Heaven was revealed after the life of David, throughout the intertestamental period, and during the development of the New Testament in the first century. Yet now, as we look at Psalm 23 in light of New Testament revelation we can see the truth of this final thought.

Part of focusing on the future is remembering that something far greater than what God has in store for you in this life is waiting for you. The word, *"Heaven,"* is found 276 times in the New Testament alone. Listen to these descriptions of Heaven with me.

The first is found in Isaiah 64:4 and repeated by Paul in 1 Corinthians 2:9, *"No eye has seen, no ear has heard, and no mind has imagined what God has prepared for those who love Him."*

Heaven is an amazing place, look how the Bible describes it:

- You will enjoy everlasting life – John 3:16

- Jesus is preparing a place for you – John 14:2

- It's a city designed and built by God. – Hebrews 11:10

- The walls are made of jasper, the main street is pure gold, like clear glass – Revelations 21:18

- The glory of God will illuminate it – Revelation 21:23

- There will be no more tears, pain, sorrow, or separation – Revelation 21:4

- Death will be conquered – Revelation 20:6

- We will enjoy the presence of Jesus – 1 John 3:2

Randy Alcorn, best-selling author of over 50 books, wrote what many Christian leaders believe to be one of our generation's great descriptions of Heaven in 2004. It's a fantastic read of over 500 pages and puts the reality of Heaven onto the written page.

In it he notes, "What we love about this life are the things that resonate with the life we were made for. The things we love are not merely the best this life has to offer—they are previews of the greater life to come."[17]

Friend, God has so much more in store for you. I hope you don't miss Heaven. If we're not careful, we let the enemies of our soul steal away the future God has for us. Alcorn continues by writing, "Nothing is more often misdiagnosed than our homesickness for Heaven. We think that what we want is sex, drugs, alcohol, a new job, a raise, a doctorate, a spouse, a large-screen television, a new car, a cabin in the woods, a condo in Hawaii. What we really want is the person we were made for, Jesus, and the place we were made for, Heaven. Nothing less can satisfy us."[18]

If you're anxious today, let me encourage you to set your mind on the things above. Also, know that you're not alone. Many followers of Jesus have utilized this last principle to make it through the tough seasons of life. Look how the apostle Paul shares this same truth with his new congregation in Colossae. *"Since you have been raised to new life with Christ, set your sights on the realities of heaven, where Christ sits in the place of honor at God's right hand. ²Think about the things of heaven, not the things of earth. ³For you died to this life, and your real life is hidden with Christ in God. ⁴And when Christ, who is your life, is revealed to the whole world, you will share in all His glory."* (Colossians 3:1-4)

This is what it means to focus on your future. We have learned four ways to overcome our anxiety through the principles found in Psalm 23. They are by… Knowing the Shepherd, Embracing the Valley, Ignoring your Enemies, and Focusing on your Future.

These four strategies will help you the next time you're anxious and you feel you're surrounded, and life is closing in on you. Remember God is great, and you will overcome as you trust in Jesus.

For some of you, the peace of God continues to escape you. The reason for this is you don't yet know the person of peace and His name is Jesus. The way to experience God's presence is to come home to Him today.

If you're completely honest at this moment you know you're lost. You've been seeking, you've been searching, you've tried many things this world has to offer and the anxiety and worries and fears of life still follow you. The way to find healing is to come home to Jesus. Yet, I know what some of you are thinking: I'm lost, and I don't know how to find the way home. My life is wrecked. I've been down too many dark alleys and crooked paths, and I don't know if God would even want to be with a person like me. Let me tell you something, not only does God want to be with you, but He is also coming for you! He will walk down the darkest trail to find you. He will traverse over the greatest canyon to rescue you. He will even go through the valley of the shadow of death alongside you. And guess what else? He's already paid the ultimate price to save you. The question for you is, have you opened your heart to receive His love for you? If not, you can do that right now.

Let me share a final story with you.

In Houston Texas, on Wednesday, October 6th, 2021, as Araceli Núñez, unloaded groceries from the family's truck, her son, Christopher played nearby. He followed a neighbor's dog into the woods, and soon after, the dog returned. But the little boy was gone.

Maybe you've lost a child for a few minutes and have experienced the adrenaline that overtakes you and the fear that grips your heart. You can imagine what Araceli was feeling at that moment.

Within a day, more than 150 law enforcement officials, FBI agents, and volunteers were searching the woods for this 3-year-old boy.

Christopher's mother pleaded for help. "Please return my child to me," Núñez said. "It's been a long time; I don't know what to do anymore. ... I'm desperate." More than 48 hours later, hope was fading.

Quiet Heart (Ps 23)

That Friday night, Tim Halfin was in his LifeGroup when he heard a number of people talking about Christopher. Tim said, "During our prayer for this little boy, the Holy Spirit spoke to me. 'Tomorrow morning, go look for him,' and I did."

Halfin joined the search team just before noon on Saturday. While they were searching, he heard the faint sound of a child's voice.

He called the sheriff's deputies over, and they found Christopher.

"I think God had been protecting this little boy all along," Tim said. "I think Jesus had been talking to him for three nights and now going on four days."

As a believer, Halfin said he always knew God could perform miracles; he'd read about them all throughout Scripture. But now he was able to be part of one by listening to God's voice.

Christopher's mom was filled with joy when she got word her boy was found alive. This is what it's like for God when one of his lost kids comes home.

If you're lost today, God is looking for you. Are you ready to come home today? Are you ready to be rescued?

Chapter 3

The Color of Hope

Psalm 27

W e're always hopeful for a new beginning when the sun rises and things start over again. Hope has a way of adding vibrant colors to a gray and sometimes depressing world.

In the 1993 film, Groundhog Day, a TV weatherman, played by actor and comedian Bill Murray, gets stuck reliving the same bad day, over and over, and over, again!

The movie was so successful that when someone says, "It feels like Groundhog's Day," they're not referring to the once-a-year event in Punxsutawney, Pennsylvania… (where they look to see if the groundhog sees his shadow) …they are actually referring to a depressing pattern, where we live out the same problems and dullness of life over and over again.

Perhaps you are in a time like that in your life? As you read this you have the chance to break the patterns of depression as we explore Psalm 27.

If you're facing a time of depression, in the hope-filled passage of Psalm 27, you'll discover four truths to help you add a splash of color to your Groundhog Day.

How many people face this issue?

A recent study by Gallup showed that 29% of Americans have been diagnosed with depression during their lifetime. In 2023, among young adults, depression has seen an increase due to social isolation and difficulties of feeling a part of a community.[19]

Can depression strike anyone, even a Christian?

It sure can. In Diana Gruver's 2020 book, "Companions in the Darkness: Seven Saints who Struggled with Depression and Doubt", she writes about well-known Christian leaders who dealt with depression in their personal life. Leaders such as Martin Luther, Charles Spurgeon, and Mother Teresa are a few of those she studied. Her research was surprising because of the many first-hand accounts of their struggles with depression.

For example, Charles Spurgeon (perhaps the greatest preacher since the Apostle Paul) once wrote, "I, of all men, am perhaps the subject of the deepest depression at times. I am the subject of depression so fearful that I hope none of you ever get to such extremes of wretchedness as I go to…although my joy is greater than most men, my depression is such as few can have an idea of."[20]

What about biblical characters?

Even famous people from the Bible experienced depression, just like many of us do. King David, a major hero from the Old Testament, wrote about his own struggles with depression. He asked a question many of us ask when we're feeling down: *"Why am I discouraged? Why is my heart so sad?"* (Ps 42:5)

Has that ever happened to you? Have you ever felt that way? Have you ever asked that type of question? If you have, you're not alone and you don't have to feel bad about it. Depression can happen to anyone, but God hasn't left us without a plan to help us overcome it.

Even though depression was a difficult problem for David to deal with, and he didn't understand why he felt that way, he found a way to climb out of the dark pit of despair, and today we'll learn how he did it.

First, we overcome depression by ...

Declaring the Truth. *"The LORD is my Light and my Salvation—so why should I be afraid? The LORD is my Fortress, protecting me from danger, so why should I tremble?"* (Psalm 27:1)

Confusion, mistrust, fear, and depression thrive in the world of deceit. The world of untruth is the devil's playground. It's the space he enjoys. It's a specialty of the world of darkness, the world of gray.

Have you ever heard of the Portia spider?

It's a master predator whose chief weapon is deception, and it uses that deception to go after other spiders. It looks like a piece of dried leaf or foliage blown into a web. When it attacks another species of spider, it uses a variety of methods to lure them into striking range. Sometimes it crawls onto the web and taps the silken threads in a manner that mimics the vibrations of a mosquito or other insect caught in the web. The unaware spider marches up for dinner and instead becomes a meal itself.

The Portia spider can tailor its deception for its prey. They can find a signal for just about any spider by trial and error. It makes different signals until the victim spider finally responds. Like the Portia spider, Satan's weapon of choice for you is deception.

In describing the devil, Jesus said, *"He has always hated the truth, because there is no truth in him. When he lies, it is consistent with his character; for he is a liar and the father of lies."* (John 8:44)

We learn from Paul that, *"Satan disguises himself as an angel of light."* (2 Corinthians 11:14)

There is an old story about the devil offering his tools for sale because he decided to go out of business. He displayed his various tools. Things like hatred, anger, jealousy, deceit, and bitterness, all had prices marked on them. But one of them was set apart and marked with a higher price than the others. When asked why this particular tool was marked so high, the devil said, "Because this is my most useful tool; it is called depression. With it, I can do anything with people that I want."

The best way to fight depression is with truth. That's what David does in Psalm 27. He declares three truths in this verse. He says, *"The Lord is my Light, my Salvation, and my Fortress."*

What is David establishing here in his life?

He's saying that God is my Light. Meaning… God is my direction. 1 John 1:5 tells us, *"This is the message we heard from Jesus and now declare to you: God is Light, and there is no darkness in Him at all."* Jesus said, *"I am the Light of the world. If you follow Me, you won't have to walk in darkness, because you will have the Light that leads to life."* (John 8:12)

Light always dispels darkness. It's never the other way around. Light always allows you to see and go in the right direction.

Next, David declares that God is my Salvation. Meaning… God is my rescue. Psalm 107:6 reminds us, *" 'LORD, help!' they cried in their trouble, and He rescued them from their distress."* If you're looking for rescue from your problems outside of Jesus, you're looking in the wrong place. When you cry for help be sure to put the LORD in front of it.

Finally, David announces that God is my fortress. Meaning… God is my place of safety. Proverbs 18:19 says, *"The name of the LORD is a strong fortress; the godly run to Him and are safe."* In the book of Revelation, when speaking to the church in Philadelphia, Jesus said, *"You obeyed my message and endured. So, I will protect you from the time of testing everyone in all the world must go through."* (Revelation 3:10 CEV). If Jesus will protect His followers from the judgment of the Great Tribulation, then He is more than capable of protecting you now. The Bible teaches us that Jesus is your place of protection.

Because God is my direction, rescue, and place of safety, David concludes… *"Why should I be afraid"* and *"Why should I tremble?"* In other words, I won't!

One of the ways to defeat depression is to declare the truth.

What's the second way to overcome depression?

Dealing with Reality. *"When evil people come to devour me,*

*when my enemies and foes attack me, they will stumble and fall.
³Though a mighty army surrounds me; my heart will not be
afraid. Even if I am attacked, I will remain confident."* (Psalm
27:2-3)

One of the things I appreciate about the Bible is just how real
it is. It doesn't sugarcoat life. It describes life as it is. In verses 2
and 3, David is describing how life has been for him. David
spent a good portion of his time running for his life. Many of
those times have been recorded for us in the book of Psalms, 1st
& 2nd Samuel, 1st Kings, and 1st Chronicles. We have a pretty
good idea of what life was like for David when he was on the
run. We know how he processed it, how he recovered from it,
and how he rose above it.

In Psalm 27, we find a summary of David's thoughts, which
was most likely written prior to his being anointed as King of
Israel. Meaning this passage was fresh off the battlefield. This
wasn't a waning story written by David at the end of his life.
This is what it felt like at the time. This is what it was like at that
moment. It's real, it's raw, authentic.

He deals with the reality that evil people want to devour him.
He has a host of enemies and foes attacking him. He includes a
mighty army that surrounds him. All of these things are
formidable foes attempting to destroy his life. David is dealing
with reality.

If you're going through depression, it's okay. It's real for you
and there's nothing wrong with you, ok? We go through battles
because we are human. Sometimes we have an enemy coming
after us. Sometimes we have evil people trying to harm us.

Sometimes it feels like there is a mighty army surrounding us. When that is happening it can feel overwhelming, out of control, scary, and discouraging. If left unchecked, it can lead to feelings of depression.

It's part of the human experience. It happened to David, it has happened to historical figures, biblical all-stars, and many people along with you. But here's the good news, one of the first steps in recovering from depression is to get real with it. We don't have to sweep it under the rug, run from it, hide from it, or be embarrassed by it. The way out of it is to go through it.

Many psychologists and psychiatrists agree that depression is caused by a combination of factors; sometimes physical, sometimes emotional, sometimes psychological, or a combination of all of them.

I'm not a physician, I'm a pastor. So, I want to say that if you feel you're not able to get through what you're going through, it's okay to seek out professional medical help in this area. In my opinion it's no different than if you or I had a heart condition and went to the best cardiologist in the area to help us.

The mind is an organ just like any other organ in our body. We have well-trained and highly qualified people in our area who can help us when we need it.

Now from my understanding of the topic, major depression is characterized by a persistent feeling of sadness or a lack of interest in outside motivation. Symptoms can vary from mild to severe for more than two weeks and include the following [21]

- Feeling sad or having a depressed mood

- Loss of interest in activities once enjoyed

- Changes in appetite, weight loss or gain unrelated to dieting

- Trouble sleeping or sleeping too much

- Loss of energy or increased fatigue

- Feeling worthless or guilty

A good friend of mine who is a licensed family therapist shared with me how she helps her clients. "I find that people who suffer from depression have very negative self-talk, can be highly self-critical, and make assumptions. It is helpful for people to ask themselves specific questions about how they are feeling. Am I feeling lonely? Am I struggling in a job where I feel overwhelmed? Do I feel like I am not measuring up? Being more specific with oneself or slicing it thinner helps address the problem and the feeling surrounding it. Feelings do matter, but they are not who you are. You are a creation of God. You are priceless, a treasure, and you are loved."[22]

Regardless of the type of depression you may be facing, there is a way out. I love how David puts it. Through all of his moments of depression, David remained confident, *"Even if I am attacked, I will remain confident."* (v 3)

The word "confident" is a Hebrew word [בָּטַח, bâṭach] and it is pronounced "baw-takh." It is connected to the idea of hope and trust. We find a similar thought in the life of the prophet Jeremiah when he writes, *"Blessed are those who trust in the LORD and have made the LORD their hope and confidence."* (Jeremiah 17:7)

Whether your way out of depression is through natural ways or medical assistance, keep your hope and trust in God. In other words, it's ok to deal with the reality of your depression and simultaneously keep your confidence in God.

What's the third way to overcome depression?

Deciding on what is Important. *"The one thing I ask of the LORD—the thing I seek most—is to live in the house of the LORD all the days of my life, delighting in the LORD's perfections and meditating in His temple."* (Psalm 27:4)

It's not a surprise for you to hear me say that much of life is about making decisions. But not just making any decisions, it's about making the right decisions. Sometimes we're down in the dumps on account of the decisions we make. If we're not careful we can put ourselves into a dreary state.

We just covered the idea that in severe cases of depression it may be the case that our depression is coming from something outside of our control. But that doesn't mean when depression first hits us, we can't take a quick inventory to see what part our decisions may have played in the whole situation. How are the priorities of my life lining up with a biblical worldview?

I heard about a man who went to see a psychiatrist one time and he said, "Doctor, I am terribly depressed." The doctor said, "Well, how bad is it?" He said, "I'm so depressed I can't get out of bed, and when I do, I can't function. I'm not eating, I'm not sleeping, I can't even put two thoughts together."

The doctor said, "Well, I know exactly what you need to do." He said, "I want you to take a trip and go anywhere you want to go." The man said, "Well, I just got back from Hawaii." The doctor said, "Then let me suggest that you go out and buy a brand-new car." The man said, "I just bought a $150,000 Mercedes Benz." The doctor said, "Well, maybe you ought to go out and build a brand-new home." The man said, "I just bought a million-dollar house."

The doctor said, "Let me get this straight. You just got back from Hawaii, you drive a Mercedes Benz, and you live in a million-dollar home." The Dr. asked, "Why are you so depressed?" The man said, "Well, I make $100 a week."

In verse four David is going to teach us something about priorities in life and how having the right priorities can help us defeat depression. He starts off by limiting or focusing his entire life down to one thing. He distills away the unimportant, the unnecessary, and the things that hold a person back. What remains is one thing and one thing only. He writes, *"The one thing I ask of the LORD—the thing I seek most."* Have you ever done that before? Have you ever sifted through what matters most in life?

Have you ever sat down in a time of prayer, meditation, or journaling and asked yourself that question? If you did that today, took 30 minutes, tuned everything out, and focused your attention on this one question, what would your answer be?

What is the one thing you would ask of God? What is the thing you seek most? It's an interesting set of questions because it reveals the motivation of your heart. Jesus told us, *"Wherever your treasure is, there the desires of your heart will also be."* (Matthew 6:21)

What do you treasure? What do you value most? When David asked these questions, even in the midst of his despair and depression, he concluded three things:

He wanted to…

Live in the house of the LORD. This is the idea that David valued, living his life in a way that matched biblical values and decisions. In other words, when faced with a decision on how to raise kids, how to handle social issues, and how to live godly in a world of ungodly people…David says he wants to do it God's way. He wants to *"Live"* in the house of the LORD. It's about living day to day in a way that honors Jesus.

Delight in the LORD's perfections. I love this part because it's about theology. Increasingly this topic is becoming more and more important. As our culture continues to drift further from a biblical worldview, an understanding of God and biblical Christianity it will become increasingly more important for us to articulate a biblical worldview to our kids, family, friends, and community. David is saying that he wants to understand who God is. He wants to know God's character and nature.

Meditate in His temple. This third part completes the circle for us as people. First, he wants to live for God. Next, he wants to understand God. Third, he wants to be with God. We are human beings, not human doings. If we're not careful, we can get caught up in performance for God, "doing things for God," and if we do that, then we will miss out on a relationship with God.

I can't promise you a perfect life, but I can say if you value this one thing, if this is what you seek, you'll be well on your way to holding off despair and/or defeating it completely.

What's the final way to defeat depression?

Deferring my concerns to God. *"For He will conceal me there when troubles come; He will hide me in His sanctuary. He will place me out of reach on a high rock. [6] Then I will hold my head high above my enemies who surround me. At His sanctuary I will offer sacrifices with shouts of joy, singing and praising the LORD with music."* (Psalm 27:5, 6)

David teaches us one final thing about dealing with depression and despair. He shares this idea of deferring our concerns, our worries, and our problems to God.

What are we learning here? Along with understanding the reality of our depression and focusing on the "one thing" we seek most (which is God), we need to defer our concerns to Him. Notice that David trusts in God to do three things, and because God is handling his concerns, it drives David to a response; *"He will"* and then *"I will"*.

One of the most dangerous things you can do if you are depressed is to pull down the shades of self-pity over your heart, crawl up in your own cocoon, and isolate yourself.

Martin Luther said, "Isolation is poison for the depressed person. For through this, the devil attempts to keep him in his power."

Someone once asked Karl Menninger, the famous psychiatrist: "What would you advise a person who is experiencing deep depression and unhappiness?" Well, they thought he would say, "Go see a psychiatrist." But here's what he said: "If you're really severely depressed, do this: Lock the door behind you, go across the street, find somebody that's in need, and do something to help them." Great advice.

Remember in verse two, the *"evil people"*, the *"enemies"*, and the *"mighty army"* surrounding him? What can we do about that? You may have noticed David is not chasing after his concerns. He's not worried about his worries. The action in this passage is dependent upon God. And the same is true for your life. God will keep you. God will protect you. God will take your concerns. Jesus will bear your burdens.

He promised it, *"If you are tired from carrying heavy burdens, come to Me and I will give you rest."* (Mat 11:28 CEV)

You don't have to carry the weight of your problems anymore. You can bring them to God.

Our job is to keep our eyes looking toward Heaven. That's what the Bible teaches, *"We are powerless before this vast army that comes against us. We do not know what to do, but our eyes are upon you."* (2 Chronicles 20:12 BSB)

Once you have given your concerns over to God, He will conceal you from trouble, He will hide you in His presence and place you out of reach from your enemies. Once you have committed those things to God, let go and let God go to work on your behalf.

I have heard it said, "The eagle that soars in the upper air does not worry itself how to cross the river."

A famous writer once penned, "When you have accomplished your daily tasks, go to sleep in peace; God is awake."[22]

If we spend less time worrying about what's happening to us and more time completing what God has for us, then we eliminate the power of our problems.

The final part of this last verse shows us David's response.

I will...

"Hold my head high"

"Offer sacrifices of joy and worship"

David's internal perspective changed, and his outward countenance followed. His soul was no longer downcast. His heart was no longer sad. His head was no longer looking down. His head was lifted as he lifted his voice. His soul burst forth in worship because no matter what surrounded him, he was with God and when you're in God's presence, joy fills your soul.

Let God pull you into His presence, minister to your soul, and then shift your focus to serving others instead of chasing after your problems. When David followed this simple step, it brought joy to his heart and music to his soul. It will do the same for you as well.

If you are of a certain age, the photograph is etched in your mind. A little boy playing under his father's desk. But this wasn't just any office, it was the oval office. The desk, Resolute.

The little boy, the son of an American President. They called him John John.

It was an optimistic moment in American life. The White House was occupied by a man with good looks and charisma, his beautiful wife, a little girl and boy. One week after the

Presidency ended in tragedy, Theodore White wrote a Life magazine article in which he wrote a phrase that defined the Kennedy era. "For a moment," he wrote, "there was Camelot."

John John grew up to be John, Jr. He earned a law degree, founded a magazine and was well on his way to establishing his own identity. Then July 16, 1999, happened.

While flying his wife and sister-in-law to a family wedding in a small plane, Kennedy experienced what is known as spatial disorientation while descending over water at dusk and lost control. His plane crashed into the Atlantic Ocean. He was only certified to fly under visual flight rules (VFR). At the time of the crash, the weather and light conditions were such that basic landmarks were obscured, making visual flight challenging. Everything was gray.

John Kennedy, Jr's life and the lives of his passengers ended when he could no longer tell up from down.

It's quite the metaphor isn't it. Maybe you have experienced periods of gray, where nothing made sense, God felt absent, and life didn't feel worth living. We get stuck in the same Groundhog Day of gray. But that's when we remember the flight plan and regain our bearings. That's when we remember we are never left alone.

When our limited human perceptions see our surroundings as gray, the reality is our future is still in full color. God is still working. His presence is still with us. And God and His Word will outlast the temporary gray out.

That's why we set our eyes on God's promises when we can't

see Him. You can trust Him to turn your gray into the full potential of colorful richness He has for your tomorrows.

Chapter 4

Strength Disguised

Psalm 121

W e all have strengths and weaknesses. Some are visible, some hidden. Did you know the world's record for brute strength is held by a tiny beetle? This mean-looking but small beetle is called the Horned Dung Beetle. Although his job is smelly, the Horned Dung Beetle sits on top of the pile for the biggest muscle of all arthropods. This beetle, called Onthophagus Taurus, was found to be able to pull a whopping 1,141 times its own body weight, the equivalent of a 150-pound person lifting six full double-decker buses.

God designed this insect to take piles of…well, dung…into burrows, and then the soil and microorganisms break it down into natural fertilizer. So not only does this little bug clean up a mess, but it also recycles. And while it may be small, it sure is strong.

So, what does a small little beetle have to do with your life?

According to a recent poll for the American Psychological Association, 27% of Americans reported that most days are so stressful they cannot function. They cited inflation (83%), violence and crime (75%), and the current political climate

(66%), as significant sources of stress.[23]

The poll, along with additional research, tells us that many people in our culture are facing real stress, and they're not seeing a way out of it. Some of you may feel stressed out, worn out, tired, or exhausted. Some of you may feel like you don't have the strength to go on.

I would like to share with you a hidden strength God has for you in Psalm 121. Just like our little friend who has a hidden strength far greater than it appears, if you track with me, you will discover a strength to overcome the stress of life the next time it comes your way.

The Bible reminds us, *"As pressure and stress bear down on me, I find joy in Your commands."* (Psalm 119:143)

This means that the Bible tells us that joy can be found amid the pressure and stress in life. So, what do we mean by the word, stress?

The dictionary defines stress as "physical, mental, or emotional strain or tension." What is interesting is that according to experts, some stress is actually necessary and even good—such as the physical strain we put on our muscles to make them stronger.

But normally, whenever we talk about stress, we are talking about that feeling of strain or tension, often caused by worries and troubles. This can be a serious issue for some. Stress can affect people in many ways, like making them physically ill, causing them to work harder, or making them shut down emotionally.

So, let's solve this as we dive into Psalm 121, and find the pathway forward.

First, you can overcome stress by understanding...

The Secret to Reduce Stress

Americans are always looking for a secret formula to accomplish what they want. We buy diet pills and programs, attend conferences and seminars, and get conned with get-rich-quick schemes and other nefarious 'secret' methods. But when it comes to stress, the secret to finding relief is revealed to us in the Bible. Let's start with verse one.

"*¹I lift up my eyes to the hills. From where does my help come? ²My help comes from the LORD, who made heaven and earth.*" (Psalm 121:1-2)

Psalm 121 is one of fifteen special Psalms in the Bible. These special Psalms are called the Songs of Ascents. (Ps 120-134) David wrote four, Solomon wrote one, and the other ten are unnamed. History records that fifteen steps led up from the Court of the Women to the Court of the Israelites. These steps correspond to the fifteen Songs of Ascents. On these steps the people of God would sing. Additionally, historians tell us that these fifteen Psalms are referred to as the pilgrim psalms which were sung by the Jewish people on their way to Jerusalem during their three annual feasts.[25]

According to Bible scholars, these special Psalms (songs) reflect the struggles of living peacefully among enemies and the anxiety felt when traveling to and from Jerusalem and their hometowns. So just like you and me, the people of God knew what it was like to deal with stressful situations. The traveler of Psalm 121 tells us three things:

First, when it comes to stress, our help...

Can't Be Found Outside - We read, *"I lift up my eyes to the hills."* In the Old Testament, when Psalm 121 was written, to look to the hills was a way for people to say, "I'm looking to an outside source for help." The picture here is one of a traveler heading down to Jerusalem for one of the annual feasts. He contemplates the journey. He considers the various pathways. He is cautious about the potential perils of travel during his day.

During this time mountains were considered dangerous and challenging places to be. They were home to wild animals and dangerous bandits. Rocky caves added to the dangers. Along with this, ancient pagan cultures built their temples in the mountains. While Jewish pilgrims found a sense of awe and majesty in the high altitude, there was also a sense of fear and uncertainty. It was a place of mixed emotions - fear, hope, and danger. It carried feelings of stress.

Many times, we look to things outside of ourselves to relieve our stress, and those things we look to are just as dangerous as the ancient robbers and false religions of Psalm 121.

Next, when it comes to stress, our help...

Can't Be Found Inside - Next, we read, *"From where does my help come?"* When traveling, it's natural to feel uneasy and unsure of what might happen. The traveler in this story is no exception. After looking at the hills, he then turns inward and considers where he might turn for help if something goes wrong.

He looks inside himself and wonders where he can find the strength to face challenges that come his way. It's a relatable feeling for anyone who has ever set out on a journey unsure of what lies ahead. The stress of his journey builds.

Have you ever engaged in self-talk like this? Have you talked to yourself like this traveler? When facing a stressful situation, you may have said, "Now what?" or "What am I going to do next?" Sometimes we can pump ourselves up and perhaps rally our internal person to step it up a few notches. But many times when we look inward, we know how low the fuel is. We know we are running on fumes.

He looks around. Then he looks within. Finally, he looks up!

Finally, when it comes to stress, our help. . .

Is Only Found in Heaven - The traveler ultimately concludes, *"My help comes from the LORD, who made Heaven and earth."*

To reduce stress, the secret is to look up. This means acknowledging that external factors are not the solution and internal searching will not provide guidance. Instead, we can find support and help from God by looking upwards.

The phrase *"the LORD, who made Heaven and earth"* is very interesting. At first glance, it appears to be a nice line tacked on to the end of the verse. But this is a very important phrase in the Bible. There are at least ten specific references to it and they all carry the same meaning.[24]

This statement is powerful because it declares that God created everything we know and see, and therefore we can trust

His power. It means that when we turn to God for help, we can have faith that he will not only care for us, but also has the ability to help us. God is not just the creator of everything, but also the one who keeps everything going. Dr. David Jeremiah says it this way, "We're not only coming to a God who cares, but a God who can."

It is easy to feel overwhelmed when facing a problem, especially when you're tired. But it's important to take a step back and look at things from a different perspective. Remember that the creator of the universe is in control and can help you overcome any challenge. Trust in Him and you will find relief from stress.

Second, I can overcome stress by understanding…

The Hidden Strength from Stress

One of the most difficult and rewarding things to do is work out. How many of you do that regularly? There's a hidden strength that develops when we put pressure or stress on our muscles. Stress causes our physical body to become stronger. A similar thing happens spiritually when we face times of stress. When a stressful situation comes your way, God provides a hidden strength that rests deep inside the hearts of believers. Drawing on this hidden strength builds up your spiritual nature and will make you stronger.

In the remainder of Psalm 121, there are three ways in which stress reminds you about your hidden strength in God.

Stress reminds you that…

God Sees You - *"³He will not let your foot be moved; He who keeps you will not slumber. ⁴Behold, He who keeps Israel will neither slumber nor sleep."* (Psalm 121:3-4)

In Bible times, if your "foot slipped," that meant disaster was coming your way. We see an instance of this in the Pentateuch regarding the enemies of God, *"In due time their feet will slip. Their day of disaster will arrive."* (Deuteronomy 32:35) In Psalm 121, some translations use this phrase, *"He will not let your foot slip."* That's a pretty good translation because that's the idea here. As the people walk towards Jerusalem, their footing is important, and here we see God's promise that He will see them safely to their destination. He will not let their *"foot be moved."* They will have a sure foundation. We have the same idea in Psalms 66 and 94.

"Bless our God...who has kept our soul among the living and has not let our feet slip." (Psalm 66:8-9)

"When I thought, 'My foot slips,' your steadfast love, O LORD, held me up." (Psalm 94:18)

Even though it's a stressful time, even though they're walking down a path filled with pressure, and even though each bend in the road brings continual uncertainty, they know that God sees them and promises to direct their path on the way to Jerusalem.

The Bible also promises us that God will not sleep or slumber. This contrasts with the pagan gods of their day, who had to be roused from their sleep, *"At noon, Elijah began making fun of them. 'Pray louder!' he said. 'Baal must be a god. Maybe he's daydreaming...Or maybe he's asleep, and you have to wake him up.'"* (1 Kings 18:27 CEV)

God watches over His people, and when you're going through your time of testing, pressure, tension, or stress…know that as a follower of Jesus, He cares for you, He sees you, and He will keep you from allowing the stress to overtake you.

This brings us to another hidden strength you have…

Stress reminds you that…

God Shields You - *"⁵The LORD is your keeper; the LORD is your shade on your right hand. ⁶The sun shall not strike you by day, nor the moon by night."* (Psalm 121:5-6)

Sometimes with the big pressures of life, you never see them coming. They can hit you like a ton of bricks. When that happens, what do you do?

Perhaps you can relate to my new friend, Chippie, the parakeet. He never saw it coming. One second, he was peacefully perched in his cage singing, the next, he was sucked in, washed up, and blown over.

His problem began when his owner decided to clean his cage with a vacuum. She stuck the nozzle in to suck up the seeds and feathers in the bottom of the cage. Then the phone rang. Instinctively she turned to pick it up. She barely said hello and then it happened. Poor Chippie was gone. The bird owner gasped, put down the phone, turned off the vacuum, and opened the bag. There was Chippie—still alive but stunned—covered with heavy black dust.

She grabbed him, rushed to the bathtub, turned on the faucet, full blast, and held Chippie under the ice-cold water. So, she did what any compassionate pet owner would do: She snatched up the hair dryer and blasted the wet, shivering little bird with hot air….

A few days after the trauma, the reporter who'd initially written about the event contacted Chippie's owner to see how the bird was recovering. "Well," she replied, "Chippie doesn't sing much anymore—he just sits and stares."[25]

As you go through the stress of life, know that the Lord is your keeper. According to this passage, the phrase "by day" or "by night" simply means that there isn't a time when God is not your shield and protector. The word "protect/keep" (שָׁמַר) shâmar, [pronounced shaw-mar'] is used six times in these eight verses.

To have the Lord as your "keeper" literally means to have the Lord as your protector. During medieval times, a castle's keep was the strongest portion of the fortification and the last resort in case of a siege or attack. It was usually a fortified tower and used as a last refuge in case of an attack. This provides us with a small picture of what it means to have the Lord as your keeper during times of tension and stress.

There's one more hidden strength you have during times of pressure.

Stress reminds you that…

God Sustains You - *"⁷The LORD will keep you from all evil; He will keep your life. ⁸The LORD will keep your going out and your coming in from this time forth and forevermore."* (Psalm 121:7-8)

In this final passage, we see a comprehensive promise that

God will keep, protect, sustain, empower, and enable you to complete your journey. Listen, friend, that's a hidden strength.

Look, just like the pilgrims of Psalm 121, we all have a journey in this life.

In relation to time, days, or seasons, some journeys may be long, some short, but according to the Bible, *"It is appointed for man to die once, and after that comes judgment."* (Heb 9:27)

Job realized this when he wrote, *"You have decided the length of our lives. You know how many months we will live, and we are not given a minute longer."* (Job 14:5)

This is why so many people are under stress. They're trying to control everything around them. Trying to squeeze out every ounce of life because they're scared it'll be gone before they know it. That's why you must remember, *"You do not belong to yourselves but to God; He bought you for a price."* (1 Corinthians 6:19 GNT)

When you're feeling stressed, remember this life is not your life, it's the life Christ has given you to live out. It's a new life designed to live out His purpose to the world through you.

When you live life with this type of clarity, the creative energies of God begin to flow through your veins like never before. When stress hits you, you get a burst of spiritual ideas. Why? Because now Godly perspectives, creative concepts, or heavenly thoughts are at the top of your thinking.

The concerns of this life are overridden by the concepts of eternal life.

And you get all of this creativity to manage life…

In Spite of Your Enemies

Look how the Bible says it… God will, *"keep you from all evil."* This doesn't imply a cushioned life but rather a well-armed one. Remember Psalm 23:4, *"Even when I walk through the darkest valley, I will not be afraid, for you are close beside me."* We can expect the dark valleys, but we can face it. As fear grows, faith grows higher.

Let me put it this way, when someone hates on you, how does God want you to handle that in light of His love for that individual? When you think this way, the stress of that situation lessens and God's purpose is explored. Your thinking goes higher, and creative thoughts arrive.

You get creativity to manage life…

In Your Daily Energies

When the Bible says, *"He will keep your life,"* it means your internal person. It's the energies of life. This is the area of your soul that really needs God's help during stressful times. It's hard to describe this, but when you're around encouraging people, you know what I'm talking about. You feel uplifted, you feel energized.

Do you want to live a less stressful life? Focus on how you can give away the presence of a godly life to others. I assure you, you will have less stress.

You get creativity to manage life…

Through Your Endeavors

God will empower, *"your going out and your coming in."*

This phrase refers to all activities of a person's daily life, including going out on the pilgrimage to Jerusalem, returning home, and all their movements in between. As the people of God followed in obedience, God is saying He watches over them and will preserve their actions and activities.

When yesterday feels like today and tomorrow feels like last week we can get discouraged. We have to remind ourselves that the coming and going of life's tasks are more than meaningless actions. They are moments that are filled with divine opportunities to touch a person's life, to influence our children's future, and to set foundations for eternity. The mundane becomes missional when we bring God's purpose into those moments of life. Stress lessens as God's purpose is evaluated.

One final thing, you get creative energy to manage life…

For All of Eternity

God will sustain you, *"from this time forth and forevermore."* This final part of Psalm 121 is like a warranty from God to you. It's not a warranty that runs out, expires, or needs to be renewed either. It's a warranty that God's blessing, protection, and eternal presence will be upon the lives of those who follow Jesus. From the moment you surrender your life until the end of time and forevermore. It's unending.

If you want to sideline your stress, cut through your chaos, or pummel your pressures start thinking about eternity. When you do that, all of what God has for you begins to show up in bits and pieces within your everyday life.

Do you think Jesus was stressed out? Do you think Jesus was

worried? Do you think Jesus carried around the problems of yesterday, the day before, or from last year? I don't think He did. He was on an eternal mission in a temporal world. And when He left, He gave you and I the mandate to continue carrying out His mission. When you tap into that, stress fades away.

Strength Disguised (Ps 121)

Chapter 5

Finding Hope in a Hopeless World

Psalm 139

Mother Teresa once said, "The biggest disease today is not leprosy or cancer. It's the feeling of being uncared for, unwanted – of being deserted and alone."

Let me ask you, is Mother Teresa correct in her assessment of today's world? Well, according to Dr. Tyler VanderWeele of Harvard University, about "50 percent of Americans report being lonely." According to his research, there's no doubt about it, more and more people are feeling sad and alone.

I want to discuss this today because I believe this issue is critical for our culture. Loneliness and despair not only have a negative impact on mental health, but also on physical health. Did you know that? And it's impacting our workplace environments too. A significant number of Gen Z and Millennials have left jobs due to mental health reasons, which impact employee engagement and retention. With 75% of the global workforce being Millennials and Gen Z by 2030, addressing loneliness is crucial.[26]

The Surgeon General of the United States recently revealed that being lonely all the time can be just as bad for your health as smoking 15 cigarettes a day. His department's 2023 report entitled, "Our Epidemic of Loneliness and Isolation," warns that the physical consequences of loneliness and despair can be devastating, including a 29% increased risk of heart disease; a 32% increased risk of stroke; and a 50% increased risk of developing dementia for older adults.[27]

The sad part about despair and loneliness is it's not limited to older adults. We're seeing a rapid increase in the lives of young people as well. According to Psychology Today, "Seventy-three percent of Gen Z report feeling alone—the highest level of any generation."[28] The article goes on to explain Gen Z is the first generation in our society that has never been offline. The entire generation is younger than Google. Yet, Despite Gen Z's digital upbringing and the inevitable advances of virtual reality, artificial intelligence, and blockchain technology, Gen Z is saying they want human relationships.

From a spiritual perspective, there are two factors driving this increase in despair and loneliness. According to the 2017 ground-breaking book Meet Generation Z, author James White concludes that there's a lack of biblical foundations in our modern culture, and our younger generations are becoming increasingly leaderless. He writes, "The degree of spiritual illiteracy is simply stunning. They are not simply living in and being shaped by a post-Christian cultural context. They do not even have a memory of the gospel." He further concludes, "They have endless amounts of information but little wisdom, and virtually no mentors."[29]

Putting all this together, we are living in a society that has drifted away from God, which has led us to drift away from each other. We've become a culture of islands. This double drift has caused an emptiness in our souls. This emptiness is being seen in the recent data as loneliness and despair.

I agree with the Surgeon General's assessment, "It's hard to put a price tag, if you will, on the amount of human suffering that people are experiencing right now." Surgeon General Dr. Vivek Murthy.

Perhaps that's you today. Perhaps you're here, and you're battling loneliness or despair, and you just can't find a way out. Perhaps you're feeling isolated, and even though you're in a crowded room, you feel all alone.

Can I share with you that you don't have to stay that way? Today, because of God's help, you can find your way out.

So, what's the answer? How can you climb out of the pit of loneliness and despair?

St. Francis of Assisi wrote, "Lord, make me an instrument of thy peace; where there is hatred, let me sow love; where there is injury, pardon; where there is doubt, faith; where there is despair, hope."

The answer is to find hope in a hopeless world. And we can do that by looking into God's Word. Remember, there are no hopeless situations; there are only those who have grown hopeless about them. Without Jesus, we have a hopeless end, but with Jesus, we have an endless hope.

So, how can you overcome your despair? You can embrace hope.

If you're new to Compass, we are in the middle of a ten-week series entitled "God's Spotify Playlist." In this series, we've identified the Top Ten Psalms that relate to our Top Ten human needs. This week, we come to Psalm 139.

Psalm 139 teaches there are four reasons why you can have hope in a hopeless world.

First, you can have hope because…

God Knows You Completely

"¹O LORD, you have examined my heart and know everything about me. ²You know when I sit down or stand up. You know my thoughts even when I'm far away. ³You see me when I travel and when I rest at home. You know everything I do. ⁴You know what I am going to say even before I say it, LORD. ⁵You go before me and follow me. You place your hand of blessing on my head. ⁶Such knowledge is too wonderful for me, too great for me to understand! (Psalm 139:1-6)

One of the things we talk about a lot here at Compass is how much God loves you. That statement (God loves you) implies that He also knows you. Why? Well, in order to love something or someone, I mean truly love them, you'd have to know them, right?

The Bible isn't shy about this point, about God loving you. Now, no doubt you're aware of John 3:16. That verse clearly tells us about God's love for His creation. But not just the rocks, animals, and other things, but more specifically the creation of His people, *"For God so loved the world, that He gave His only Son, that whoever believes in Him should not perish but have eternal life."*

When Jesus died upon the cross, He didn't die for anything other than for us. More specifically for you! Did you know that? Some people find that hard to believe. They ask...

Do you mean to tell me that Jesus died for me? Yes.

Even though I'm a mess? Yes.

Even though I've done things I'm embarrassed about? Yes.

Even though I've cut off everyone around me? Yes.

Even though I've sinned and cut myself off from God? Yes.

Even though I've told God I don't want anything to do with Him? Yes.

The Bible tells us, *"God showed His great love for us by sending Christ to die for us while we were still sinners"* (Romans 5:8). You see, the word "sinner" in this verse actually means someone who's devoted to sin, not free from it, or someone who is especially wicked. In short, someone who's a hot mess.

And that's one of the main reasons you can have hope. Jesus knows you; He loves you, and He freely chose to go to the cross to pay the penalty for your sin. Listen, friend, you only give your life away to those whom you love. You only pay the penalty for those who are your own. I may like your kids, but I'm not paying their penalty for them. Now, my kids, I'm willing to go to the wall for them. Why? Because I love them. They're my kids.

You're one of God's kids. You're a part of His creation. He loves you!

Let's break this passage down. What's the main thing happening here?

In verses one through five, we read about God knowing our actions, thoughts, and activities. These comparisons of *"sitting down or standing up,"* – *"traveling or resting at home,"* – *"going before me and following after me"* are Old Testament illustrations representing routine life and affirming that God cares about the details of our life. But God's care for you goes way beyond the small details of your life. We also discover that God knows, "my heart, my thoughts, my words, literally everything about me and everything I do. Even when I'm far away and even before I say it." I'm going to go out on a limb here and say I think the Bible is trying to teach us that God knows us completely.

If you're in despair today, if you're feeling all alone, please know that God sees you. He knows what you're going through. He's here for you today. And guess what? He wants you to know Him.

If you've put yourself on an island in an attempt to get away from God, in an attempt to isolate yourself, He's telling you today the rescue boat has arrived. It's time to get off the island of loneliness and come home to Jesus today.

First, you can have hope because God knows you completely.

Next, you can have hope because…

God Is With You Fully

"⁷I can never escape from Your Spirit! I can never get away from Your presence! ⁸If I go up to heaven, You are there; if I go down to the grave, You are there. ⁹If I ride the wings of the morning, if I dwell by the farthest oceans, ¹⁰even there Your hand will guide me, and Your strength will support me. ¹¹I could ask the darkness to hide me and the light around me to become night—¹²but even in darkness I cannot hide from You. To You the night shines as bright as day. Darkness and light are the same to You." (Psalm 139:7-12)

It's one thing to be known by someone, but it's another thing to be with someone. In this second part of Psalm 139, we read about David's understanding of God's presence being with him no matter where he goes. He uses comparative terms again to illustrate the great capacity of God. It's a poetic way to explain God's greatness. In other words, there are no limitations to God's presence.

He starts with, *"⁷I can never escape from your Spirit! I can never get away from your presence! ⁸If I go up to heaven, You are there; if I go down to the grave, You are there."*

This translation (the New Living Translation) uses the word *grave*. Many translations use the word Sheol. Maybe you have bumped into that word before. It's only found in the Old Testament. In the OT, Sheol referred to the grave or the place of the dead. It's not a reference to final hell, or what Revelation 20 refers to as *"the Lake of Fire."* That opens for business after the final judgment.

From the heavens to the depths of the earth, from the east to the west, in the darkest of times to the brightest of days, God will be with you. David goes on to say, in any and all situations, *"Your hand will guide me, and Your strength will support me."* (v10) So it's not just that God will be with you. God is not just hanging out with you at In and Out Burger getting a double-double with cheese along with an oversized shake. The Bible is telling us that along with His presence, you will have guidance and support. Let me tell you what this means because it's super fascinating. It's one of the reasons I enjoy reading in the original languages.

This word, *guide,* is the Hebrew word [נָחָה nâchâh, naw-khaw'] which means to guide; by implication, to transport (into exile, or as colonists), or to bring.

This word *support,* that's connected to *"your strength will support me"* is [אָחַז 'âchaz, aw-khaz'], and it means to seize (often with the idea of holding in possession). Some translations say, "Your right hand shall hold me."

I remember when all three of our kids were learning how to walk. We would prop them up and then stand behind them, bent over a bit, and gently guide them down the hall or across the room. If they were about to fall, we'd reach out and with our hand, we would get ahold of them, and put them back up, so they could continue the journey.

Here we see this same type of beautiful picture of God bringing us to the place He has for us. Guiding as a parent guides their toddler as they learn to walk.

Isn't much of life learning how to walk through it? As you do, know that God is walking through life with you. He's guiding you and holding you up when you fall.

So, you can have hope because God knows you completely and is with you fully.

Third, you can have hope because…

God Knows You Initially

"¹³You made all the delicate, inner parts of my body and knit me together in my mother's womb. ¹⁴Thank you for making me so wonderfully complex! Your workmanship is marvelous—how well I know it. ¹⁵You watched me as I was being formed in utter seclusion, as I was woven together in the dark of the womb. ¹⁶You saw me before I was born. Every day of my life was recorded in your book. Every moment was laid out before a single day had passed. ¹⁷How precious are your thoughts about me, O God. They cannot be numbered!

¹⁸I can't even count them; they outnumber the grains of sand! And when I wake up, You are still with me! (Ps 139:13-18)

This third section of Psalm 139 is by far the most recognized, especially verses 13 and 14. The Bible points out in this section that God has equipped you for a mission only you can accomplish. It means God has a plan for you. God has a purpose for you. God planned all of this before you were even born. Look at verse 16, *"You saw me before I was born. Every day of my life was recorded in your book. Every moment was laid out before a single day had passed."*

101

Finding Hope (Ps 139)

This passage in the Bible provides one of the most succinct and clearest understandings of the biblical view that human life begins at conception. If you've ever doubted what God's view is on when human life begins, the place to start is Psalm 139:13-16. It even goes a bit further than conception with an indication that prior to the beginning of your human life, God knew every moment and every day of your life. I think that's pretty cool. This is one of the reasons to have hope. You have a divine purpose.

There are many factors that contribute to the rise of loneliness and despair in our society. Those factors include an increase in daily social media intake to the simplicity of doing many of our daily tasks through technology instead of person-to-person contact. Much of the research shows that a lack of social interaction combined with a lack of life purpose are some of the greatest factors contributing to the increase of loneliness in today's culture.

If there is one area of this message that I really want you to know about, it is this area.

To know that God knows you is one thing.

To know that God is with you is another thing.

But to know that God has a purpose for your life, that's a whole other thing.

Having a God-sized purpose for your life...

Lifts you up when you're down.

It propels you forward when you want to go backward.

It keeps you moving when you're feeling stuck.

It focuses your priorities when you don't have a plan.

It causes you to embrace your future when you're not proud of your past.

God is not done with you. He is just getting started. If you're alive, if you're breathing, if you're moving, if you're thinking… God is not done. Just because your life is in a holding pattern doesn't mean your future is in a holding cell.

Listen to how the Bible describes ten specific connections God has with you before you were even born (vs 13-18):

1. He made all the parts of your body

2. He knit you together

3. You were made wonderfully complex

4. His workmanship was marvelous

5. He watched you being formed

6. He saw you before you were born

7. Your life was pre-recorded

8. Every moment was laid out

9. His thoughts about you outnumbered the grains of sand

10. And no matter how dark or how long the night, He promised to still be with you

If God took the time and effort to do all of these things before you drew your first breath, don't you think He has some sort of purpose or design for the life you live now?

Because God has known you from your beginning, you can have hope. You're not alone, and you're not without a purpose.

God created a way for you to pursue God's purpose for your life, and you do that by getting your relationship with Jesus squared up first. In other words, if you're battling loneliness and despair and you haven't gone all in for Jesus yet, you need to start there first.

Once you've crossed over that line and the Holy Spirit is activated in your life on a day-to-day basis, then you have the right tools to fight those emotions. You have the right resources to pull your life out of that pit. You can then relate to the truth of these ten connections in a new way.

So far, we've learned that you can have hope because God knows you completely, He is with you fully, and He knew you initially.

Finally, you can have hope because…

God Rewards Your Honesty

"23Search me, O God, and know my heart; test me and know my anxious thoughts. 24Point out anything in me that offends you and lead me along the path of everlasting life." (Ps 139:23-24)

I heard a story about a husband and wife who were on a long road trip. They stopped at a full-service gas station in a small town. After the station attendant had washed their car's windshield, the husband asked, "It's still dirty, can you wash it again?" So, the attendant did. After washing it again, the husband still in the car got a little upset, "It's still dirty. Don't you know how to wash a windshield?" Seeing what was going on, his wife reached over, removed her husband's glasses from his face, and cleaned them. Then he put them back on and behold—the windshield was clean!

It's common for us to blame others for not doing their job properly, but often the issue lies with ourselves. When your perspective is clouded, everything can seem unclear and confusing. However, once you take responsibility for your own actions and work on improving yourself, the world around you becomes brighter and full of hope.

When you can see the world with fresh eyes and a clear heart, you can then best know how God wants you to understand and live out the assignment He has for you. Knowing your purpose provides hope and living out your purpose sustains hope.

David gets real with God and asks for Him to search his heart, test his motives, know his thoughts, and point out anything that is an offense to God. Let me ask you, when was the last time you did that? This is a risky proposition. Are you prepared to be that honest with God?

When you come to God and ask Him to search your heart, He will. Here's the deeper question, when He points out the thing or things that offend Him, what are you going to do about it?

You have a few options. You can pretend you didn't hear it, hang on to it, or you can be honest about it. Obviously, when we're honest about letting go of those things that are an offense to God, that's when we will see and experience God's presence in a new way. That's when hope builds in your heart.

That's when the mission of God in our life begins to take on new meaning. That's when ministry in God's kingdom becomes more exciting. When you experience God's presence in this type of way, it is special.

I mentioned that God rewards your honesty. What did I mean by that? Let me approach it this way, why do you think David is coming to God in such an honest way? David does this because he knows honesty, or loyalty, to God brings everlasting life. And everlasting life, my friend, is your ultimate hope. David concludes Psalm 139 with this hopeful request, *"Lead me along the path of everlasting life."*

Do you want that path? Then be honest with God. And watch your heart be flooded with hope like never before.

This is the first step on your way out of the pit of loneliness and despair. When God pulls you from that pit, He puts you on a new path. It's a path toward everlasting life as you live out the mission God has for you. A mission only you can fulfill. A mission uniquely designed for you. This means you have purpose. You have a reason. All of this provides new hope.

On the surface, James Harrison looks average. He loves his daughter and grandkids, collects stamps, and goes for walks near his coastal home in Australia. But it's what's under the surface that makes him extraordinary. God has uniquely designed him to accomplish a mission only he can fulfill.

Harrison is known as "The Man with the Golden Arm." Nearly every week for the past 60 years, he has donated plasma. You see, James had undergone a life-threatening medical procedure when he was a child that took 13 units of blood to save his life.

One day, he decided to donate blood and soon after, doctors contacted him. They informed him that his blood could help solve a deadly problem. In his home country of Australia, babies were dying in large numbers every year. Doctors were baffled and didn't know the reason behind it. Women were experiencing miscarriages and babies were being born with brain damage. It turned out to be a condition called Rhesus Disease which occurs when a pregnant woman's blood starts attacking her unborn baby's blood cells.

Harrison was discovered to have an unusual antibody in his blood, so he worked with doctors to use the antibodies to develop an injection called Anti-D. It prevents women with Rhesus-negative blood from developing Rh-D antibodies during pregnancy.

In short, Harrison's blood is precious. He is considered an Australian national hero and has now donated his plasma more than 1,000 times. His lifelong mission and generosity are credited with saving countless babies.[30]

Harrison's blood is precious indeed. But there is another whose blood is the most precious of all. His name is Jesus. The blood of Jesus paid the penalty for your sin and the power of His sacrifice for you can transform your life instantly. When you receive His free gift of salvation, you walk across the line from death to life.

Everlasting life isn't just for the future. Everlasting life begins the moment you give your heart and life over to Jesus. If you haven't done that yet, I want to give you the chance to do that today. When you do, you can begin the journey to live out the mission that only you can fulfill for Him on this earth.

Imagine what your life could be if you went all in for Jesus and you did it starting today.

Chapter 6

God's Answer
for a
Dopamine Generation

Psalm 51

Scaling Mt. Everest was once reserved for only a handful of elite climbers, but today over 600 people attempt it each year. However, they don't make the trek alone. The secret behind the success of those who summit can be attributed to those referred to as "The Guardian Angels of the Himalayas."

Sherpas are a special ethnic group from Nepal who have lived high up in the Himalayas for generations. To know why Sherpas are special, you have to understand that surviving a trip up Everest comes down to overcoming the atmosphere at high altitude. Hardly any humans can make the climb without added oxygen.

But after centuries at high altitude, Sherpas have mastered the ability to survive in an inhospitable atmosphere. Sherpas are more efficient at using oxygen because there are differences in the cells that generate energy. There are 30 unique differences between a Sherpa's DNA and yours or mine.

At high altitude, blood flow within small blood vessels slows down in non-Sherpas, it remains normal in them. Where others perish, they thrive. They are energized and fully alive, while others are struggling to breathe.

Unique among the people of the world, they are designed to live in the heights. They have a mission that they are uniquely qualified to fulfill.

When we hear stories like this, we get encouraged, and we know it to be true. Every one of us has a unique contribution. A unique fingerprint upon the world. A life designed to help others achieve great heights while we soar with them among the clouds of success.

But we don't all make the climb. Let's address one of the challenges plaguing so many today.

Addiction functions like a barrier that prevents you from climbing to great heights. Just when you attempt to ascend new mountains, addiction steals the air from your lungs and pulls you back down. Addiction keeps you off the mountaintop and trapped in the valley.

Those who battle addiction know the struggle. Those who have watched a loved one battle addiction know the feelings of helplessness, frustration, and pain that go along with it.

Recently, the U.S. Department of Health and Human Services released its most comprehensive report on substance use. Key findings include:[31]

- 61 million people (22% -population) used illicit drugs in

the past year.

- 46 million people (17% -population) have a substance use disorder.

- 94% of those with a substance use disorder did not receive any treatment.

What's the effect?

- Every year, alcohol kills over 95,000 Americans.

- Drug overdose causes an additional 70,000 deaths.

- Accidental drug overdose is now a leading cause of death for those under the age of 45.[32]

- The number of overdose deaths is increasing at an annual rate of 4%.

- The annual cost of substance abuse treatment is over $600 billion.[33]

Addiction is costly regarding life, finances, and relationships, and it's taking a toll on our society.

Regrettably, these statistics only cover chemical addictions, such as alcohol and drug use. However, experts warn us that there are other forms of addiction known as behavioral addictions that can be just as dangerous, devastating, and destructive. These may include addictive behaviors related to food, social media, sex, or gambling.[34]

How can you shake off the addictions of life (whether behavioral or chemical) and scale the mountains of success that God designed for you to climb?

In looking at the Top Ten Psalms from the Bible that teach us how to overcome our Top Ten Human Needs we look at things like loneliness, depression, and anxiety. Now we focus our attention on how to overcome addiction.

First, I can overcome my addiction…

Because God Is Merciful

"¹Have mercy on me, O God, according to your steadfast love; according to your abundant mercy blot out my transgressions. ²Wash me thoroughly from my iniquity and cleanse me from my sin!" (Psalm 51:1-2)

One of the things we need to remember when dealing with major problems or issues in life is that God is always wanting the best for our life. Too many people have developed a wrong perspective of God. They think God wants to crush them. They think God wants to squash them. They think God is judgmental and takes pleasure in bringing forth disapproval of their life.

We need to remember not to confuse issuing a judgment with being judgmental. Those are two different things. Issuing a judgment is based upon fairness and rightness while being judgmental is a trait connected to hypocrisy and legalism.

Because of His righteousness, God cannot be anything other than righteous. That means He looks at everything in the right way. In a way that is righteous. In a way that matches the goodness of His character. He can, therefore, properly issue the right judgment.

The Bible reminds us that, *"The LORD is ready to show you mercy; He sits on His throne, ready to have compassion on you.*

Indeed, the LORD is a just God; all who wait for Him in faith will be blessed." (Isaiah 30:18 NET)

When we compare our actions to His nature, we fall short, and unless we deal with our unrighteous actions and attitudes, God's judgment (or rightness) will bump up against our failed actions. In other words, God is the standard against which we measure our actions.

David understands this and starts out by asking God to have mercy on him. That's where we need to start too.

In your desire to overcome your addiction, this is where you start. In the original language, *mercy* is [חָנַן chânan, khaw-nan'], and it means "to be gracious, or to show favor." That's what David is asking for. He asks for God's graciousness because he knows that God's mercy is rooted in his "steadfast love" for people.

Here's the thing... God is righteous, but He also loves you because He is loving. It's a love that is steadfast, unmovable, unable to be changed, modified, or removed. Just as much as God is righteous, He is also loving. And His love is already yours. You can't buy it, earn it, or negotiate for it. Let me give you an illustration.

A little boy came to the Washington Monument and noticed a guard standing by it. The little boy looked up at the guard and said, "I want to buy it." The guard stooped down and said, "How much do you have?" The boy reached into his pocket and pulled out a dollar. The guard said, "That's not enough." The boy replied, "I thought you would say that." So, he pulled out 50 cents more. The guard looked down at the boy and said, "You need to understand three things. First, $1.50 is not enough. In fact, $150 million is not enough to buy the Washington Monument. Second, the Washington Monument is not for sale. And third, if you are an American citizen, the Washington Monument already belongs to you."

We need to understand three things about God's mercy.

- First, you cannot earn it.

- Second, it is not for sale.

- Third, when you accept Christ, you already have it.

Notice the three action verbs in Psalm 51:1-2: *blot out, wash,* and *cleanse* are specific actions God takes on your behalf because of His mercy. And it's all rooted in His deep love for you.

If you have a desire to be free from your addiction, don't think for a minute that God is not going to help you along the way. Because of His love and mercy, He will provide the tools and resources you need. You can overcome your addiction because God is merciful.

Second, I can overcome my addiction…

Because I Know My Brokenness

"³For I know my transgressions, and my sin is ever before me. ⁴Against you, you only, have I sinned and done what is evil in Your sight, so that You may be justified in Your words and blameless in Your judgment. ⁵Behold, I was brought forth in iniquity, and in sin did my mother conceive me. ⁶Behold, You

delight in truth in the inward being, and You teach me wisdom in the secret heart." (Psalm 51:3-6)

This second point is an interesting point because it is determined by the heart of the individual. In the story of Psalm 51, David, King of Israel, gets called to account by a prophet named Nathan. When he first is approached, David almost ignores him. But then, due to a little creativity by Nathan, David finally gets real. You can find the story of this interaction in 2 Samuel 11 and 12.

This point of knowing our brokenness, is so true for those going through the battle of addiction. We attempt to ignore the symptoms. Overlook the problems. Disregard the feedback of others, especially the ones we love.

It is one thing to ignore the comments of your enemies, but it is a good idea to listen to the voices of those around you who love you and have your best interest in mind. Too many times, our addiction blinds us to the truth.

David goes through a four-step process on his road to recovery.

Here it is…he

Got Real With Himself

"³For I know my transgressions, and my sin is ever before me."

We need to stop pretending everything is alright when clearly, it's not. Here's the truth, everyone is broken, just in different places. If you are broken in a way that is crying out for help, it is time to get real with yourself.

Got real with God

"⁴Against You, You only, have I sinned and done what is evil in Your sight, so that You may be justified in Your words and blameless in Your judgment."

Ultimately you and I were created by God for a purpose. When we get out of alignment with that purpose, we experience less than God's best for our life. God doesn't need to justify His actions. God doesn't need to justify His love. If we are out of alignment with God, we are the ones who need to change.

Got real with his past

"⁵Behold, I was brought forth in iniquity, and in sin did my mother conceive me."

Many of us carry a past. But don't let the past dictate your future. You may have done some things you're not proud of. Things you wished you didn't do or get involved in. But don't let that keep you from doing what God has in store for you in the days ahead. Be real with your past but be ready to move on from it.

Got real with his future

"⁶Behold, You delight in truth in the inward being, and You teach me wisdom in the secret heart."

Two of the things we need in order to move forward in life are truth and wisdom. David recognizes that these are two qualities and characteristics God is interested in. God delights when we have truth deep within, and God teaches us wisdom within the depths of our hearts when we're ready for it. If you want to move forward today in a positive way, be ready to move forward in the truth and wisdom found in God's word.

You can overcome your addiction because God is merciful, and when you know your brokenness.

Third, I can overcome my addiction…

Because God Can Restore Me

"⁷Purge me with hyssop, and I shall be clean; wash me, and I shall be whiter than snow. ⁸Let me hear joy and gladness; let the bones that you have broken rejoice. ⁹Hide your face from my sins and blot out all my iniquities. ¹⁰Create in me a clean heart, O God, and renew a right spirit within me. ¹¹Cast me not away from your presence and take not your Holy Spirit from me. ¹²Restore to me the joy of Your salvation and uphold me with a willing spirit." (Psalm 51:7-12)

In verses 7-9, we see a continued heart of repentance and sorrow from David. In verses 10-12, we see a transformation taking place. The main point here is God's ability to restore a person's life. But not just any person, a broken person. We tend to think that our life is ruined and over when we face the consequences of our addiction. We tend to think that our brokenness leads to a final defeat.

Your bad decisions do not have to lead to your final defeat. God can and will use those defeats in your life to make you stronger, wiser, and better equipped to face the challenges ahead when you come to Him.

In the 1995 movie, Apollo 13, the story of the almost disastrous mission to the moon was lived out on screen. It was very dramatic. During the mission, a NASA team member told Gene Kranz, the commander in charge, that "This could be the worst disaster NASA's ever faced." Kranz disagreed and said, "With all due respect sir, I believe this is going to be our finest hour." And it was.

We tend to think of victories as life's finest hours, but the opposite is often true. Trials and tribulations call for faith, perseverance, repentance, and restoration in ways that victory never will. In any kind of failure you experience, you can have the finest hour because of God's grace. When you bring your heart to Jesus, He will heal it and restore it. He will remake it and reshape it. Look at these biblical examples.

In Luke 15, the prodigal son, after wasting his inheritance on crazy poor choices, returned to his father's house broken and repentant. His father, rather than rejecting him, forgave and restored him.

A life caught up in addiction is much like a precious vessel that falls and shatters into many pieces. The owner, *being God*, rather than discarding it, carefully gathers all the pieces and painstakingly mends it. The repaired vessel, bearing the marks of its previous fracture displays the skill and care of the one who restored it. This beautifully illustrates Psalm 51:8, *"Let me hear joy and gladness; let the bones that you have broken rejoice."*

In another part of the Old Testament, the prophet Jeremiah describes how God, like a potter with clay, can remake and reshape us according to His will, despite our flaws or mistakes,

"⁴But the jar he was making did not turn out as he had hoped, so he crushed it into a lump of clay again and started over...⁶can

I not do to you as this potter has done to His clay? As the clay is in the potter's hand, so are you in my hand." (Jeremiah 18:4-6)

All throughout the pages of the Bible, we read and hear the stories of men and women God has restored. All throughout the pages of history, we read and hear about the same types of stories…lives being restored. Throughout the story of your life, you've seen and experienced the same truth in the lives of those around you. God is in the restoration business.

There's a reason God does this. Would you like to know what it is? In Paul's letter to the restored Christians in the city of Corinth, he writes, *"We now have this light shining in our hearts, but we ourselves are like fragile clay jars containing this great treasure. This makes it clear that our great power is from God, not from ourselves."* (2 Corinthians 4:7)

God restores you so that He can shine through you!

This brings us to our final reason.

Finally, I can overcome my addiction…

When My Life Reflects Him

"13 Then I will teach transgressors your ways, and sinners will return to you. 14 Deliver me…and my tongue will sing aloud of Your righteousness. 15 O Lord, open my lips, and my mouth will declare Your praise…17 The sacrifices of God are a broken spirit; a broken and contrite heart, O God, You will not despise." (Psalm 51:13-17)

At the end of Psalm 51, we hear David's desire to reflect God's graciousness to him, and to the world. He mentions his desire to teach, sing, and declare the goodness of God. The effect of his reflection on God's grace in his life is that others, those who are far off from God, will return to Him.

This is the beautiful thing about your life when God restores you. He then takes your life and uses it to impact those who need it. Many times, it will be the same people who are battling the struggle from which God delivered you. He does that because we connect with those who have gone through what we're going through.

I want to impress upon you that if you're in a battle right now, if you're in the middle of a strong struggle, first know that you're not alone. Next, know that God is more than able to deliver you. Finally, know that if you stick with God and allow Him to take you through a time of restoration, on the other side of that experience, He will use your life as a blessing to others.

Part of the journey to overcome addiction will be reflecting the life of Jesus in our day-to-day life. What do I mean by that? As God is working in you, as you learn more about the tools and resources available for you, as you get better connected with those who can help you, as you get real about your situation with God and the ones you love, all of this comes together like individual pieces of a giant puzzle. As you work on putting those pieces together, this reflection part is like fuel to the engine.

Let me share three quick ways you can reflect Jesus:

Love others unconditionally. Jesus taught and showed love for all, even His enemies. Try to be patient, kind, and understanding with everyone you meet. 1 John 4:7 says, *"Beloved, let us love one another, for love is from God, and* *whoever loves has been born of God and knows God."*

Serve others. Jesus led by serving others. He washed His disciples' feet and healed the sick. Find ways to put the needs of others before your own. Mark 10:45 says, *"For even the Son of Man came not to be served but to serve, and to give His life as a ransom for many."*

Practice humility. Despite being the Son of God, Jesus was not prideful. Follow His example by not seeking personal recognition or glory. Philippians 2:5-8 says, *"Have this mind among yourselves, which is yours in Christ Jesus, who, though He was in the form of God, did not count equality with God a thing to be grasped, but emptied Himself, by taking the form of a servant..."*

In other words, you can't help but love people when you love them like Jesus does. You can't help but serve people when you serve them like Jesus would. You can't help but be humble and rest on His grace when you practice humility the way Jesus lived that out.

Keep in mind that reflecting the life of Jesus doesn't mean being perfect but striving each day to be more Christ-like in all your actions. If you just focus on one of these qualities of Jesus this week, over the next three weeks, you'll begin to see a positive movement away from your addiction and toward a better life with God.

Redirecting your desire helps to deliver you from your addiction.

In the 1960's one book sold over 15 million copies, becoming a massive bestseller. In 1970 the book was turned into a movie which, once again, became a hit. The book was The Cross and the Switchblade, and the author was a young pastor from rural Pennsylvania named David Wilkerson.

It was February 28, 1958, when 26-year-old Wilkerson, touched by an article he read in Life Magazine, made an eight-hour drive from his quiet mountain village to downtown Manhattan to speak to seven accused gang members about Jesus.

Wilkerson befriended Nicky Cruz, a member of the Mau Maus street gang, and other gang members. It was an unlikely pairing, only something the Holy Spirit could orchestrate.

He led many of them to a personal relationship with Jesus Christ. He also realized their addiction to drugs was keeping them enslaved in a deadly lifestyle. So, in 1960, Wilkerson opened a center called Teen Challenge, to treat those struggling with addiction. Troubled youth poured in.

One skeptical psychiatrist observing the program remarked, "It seems to me you're just using Jesus as a crutch." "Then give me two of them," a resident of the center responded. "What is the program?" the psychiatrist asked. "God in the morning, Jesus in the afternoon, and the Holy Ghost at night," the resident replied.

Flash forward. Today, Teen Challenge operates over 1,400 affiliate centers in 129 countries, with one of the highest addiction recovery success rates anywhere in the world. In fact, a recent study showed that an astonishing 78% of graduates from Adult & Teen Challenge addiction recovery centers remain sober and substance-free post-graduation.

What started with one young man reading an article and being prompted to do something about it became a worldwide movement to save lives.

In the same way, God is impressing each of us to be His hands and feet, and rescue others from addiction and from the habits destroying their lives. And all we have to do is say, "Yes" to God, give in to the prompting of the Holy Spirit, and put the car in drive. God will reveal Himself to us each step of the way.

God's Answer (Ps 51)

Chapter 7

Anger Management: Defeating the Rapid Blaze Within

Psalm 46

Benjamin Franklin once said, "Anger is never without a reason, but seldom with a good one."

Proverbs 26:21 reminds us, *"A quarrelsome person starts fights as easily as hot embers light charcoal or fire lights wood."*

There's no doubt that anger or rage can ignite quickly and turn into a roaring blaze wreaking havoc and leaving destruction in its path.

In the spring of 1894, the Baltimore Orioles came to Boston to play a routine baseball game. But what happened that day was anything but routine. The Orioles John McGraw got into a fight with the Boston first baseman Tommy Tucker. Within minutes all the players from both teams had joined in the brawl. The fighting quickly spread to the grandstands. Among the fans, the conflict went from bad to worse. Someone set fire to the stands and the entire ballpark burned to the ground. Not only that, but the fire spread to 107 other Boston buildings as well.

Someone once said, "Getting angry can sometimes be like leaping into a wonderfully responsive sports car, stepping on the gas, taking off at high speed, and then discovering the brakes are out of order."

Maybe that's happened to you before. You let the hair-trigger emotion of anger get the best of you. I think we can all confess to a time or two where anger got the best of us. But the good news is that you don't have to live your life under the power of anger.

In God's Spotify Playlist we tackle some of the toughest things life throws at us. We look at overcoming depression, loneliness, fear, and many other important areas. What we will discover is that God has uniquely designed the Bible to help us with each one of ten major issues that we face.

That's why we are looking at the "Top Ten Psalms" in the Bible that relate to the Top Ten pressing human needs in our lives.

The topic of anger is important because emotion is fundamental to the human experience, and your reactions to emotions like anger play a crucial role in shaping the life you create.

So, what is anger? Anger is "an emotional state that varies in intensity from mild irritation to intense fury and rage," according to Charles Spielberger, PhD, a psychologist who specializes in the study of anger. He writes, "Like other emotions, it is accompanied by physiological and biological changes; when you get angry, your heart rate and blood pressure go up, as do the levels of your energy hormones, adrenaline and noradrenaline."[35]

Sadly, according to the data, we're seeing high levels of anger in our culture today. Many people feel threatened by changes in society, loss of economic and relational control, along with political differences deemed harmful to their life. All of this has led to increasing rates of anger, anxiety, and aggression. We live in a country where people are very mad at each other. In fact, in 2022 America someone was shot and killed in a road rage incident every 16 hours.[36]

Hopefully no one reading this will be put in that type of situation or let their anger take them down the road of that type of response, but how many times have you let your anger get the best of you?

If left unchecked and out of control, anger will redirect the course of your life and the lives of those around you. It will take you down the road of regret, a dead-end road.

The question today is, how can you best get ahold of anger and minimize its negative impact on your life?

We can answer that question by looking at our next Top Ten Psalm… Psalm 46.

First, I can overcome my anger/reactions…

With the Wisdom of God's Presence

"¹God is our refuge and strength, always ready to help in times of trouble*. ²So we will not fear when earthquakes come and the mountains crumble into the sea. ³Let the oceans roar and foam. Let the mountains tremble as the waters surge!" (Psalm 46:1-3)

*Trouble = distress, affliction, adversity, anguish, tribulation, adversary.

Psalm 46 was written by the Sons of Korah, a group of musicians and singers in the Old Testament. It's part of a collection of psalms called the "Songs of Zion." (Psalms 46-48) These psalms celebrate the security, power, and presence of God in Jerusalem.

Prior to the writing of these psalms of celebration, the city of Jerusalem was facing great danger. In 701 BC, the Assyrian king Sennacherib invaded Judah and laid siege to Jerusalem, threatening to conquer the city. The people were feeling scared, anxious, and angry. They wanted to do something about it.

The people of God saw Jerusalem as a representation of God's presence and protection for them. In the midst of this turmoil and internal angst, the psalmist proclaims that God is our refuge and strength. This is an important declaration, as in ancient times people often sought safety in fortified cities or strongholds to protect themselves from their enemies. However, the psalmist reminds us that true protection and strength during threatening times comes from God alone.

Through God's divine presence the Assyrian King was defeated, and the people of God were delivered. You can read this story in 2 Kings 18-19, Isaiah 36-37, or 2 Chronicles 32.

Interestingly enough, this historical event was captured by the King of Assyria. It's inscribed on Sennacherib's Prism which details the events of his campaign against Judah. This was discovered in the ruins of Nineveh in 1830 and is now stored at the Oriental Institute in Chicago, Illinois.[37]

We also see this principle of God's presence bringing victory, spelled out for us in the New Testament. The Apostle Paul wrote to the young believers in Corinth that during his times of weakness, the "power," or "presence," of Christ was revealed.

What are times of weakness? Times of weakness are those moments when situations get outside of your control. It's when you can't contain the problems, the pain, or the processes of life. In those moments, when you're getting angry, when you're facing a time of injustice, irritation, or injury, you have to remember that God is not distant or incapable of helping you. You don't have to resort to anger to solve the situation.

God is always present and willing to help you, especially in your times of trouble. The Bible emphasizes this point through the life of Paul. That's why Jesus Himself had to tell Paul that his strength is made perfect in weakness. Here's what Jesus said to Paul, *"Hey Paul...My grace is all you need. My power works best in weakness."* (2 Corinthians 12:9)

This is teaching you that you can trust Jesus to be your source of strength and refuge. Anger rises when you want to take matters into your own hands, when you want to take refuge in your own strength, your own power.

It is important to understand that anger typically arises from our fight or flight response to a perceived threat. While physical threats are a natural trigger for this response, emotional and behavioral threats can also provoke it. In these situations, we may feel our ego is under attack, leading us to react with anger.

Let's go back to the text, did you notice in this first part of Psalm 46 that when the world all around you is crashing in, you don't have to panic? You don't have to be troubled. You don't have to resort to anger.

Check it out... *"When earthquakes come," "the mountains crumble," "the oceans roar,"* or *"the waters surge"* None of these things should cause you to be triggered into a reaction you'll soon regret. The Bible says, *"we will not fear."*

In other words, my situation will not move me to an unhealthy reaction. Fear, angst, panic, anxiety, and alarm have no home in my heart. When situations outside of my control come knocking at my door, and I'm tempted to invite that chaos in... the sign out front will say "No Vacancy." God is in this house! I already have a resident and He is the president of my life and His name is Jesus!

The scripture is clear, God will be your, *"refuge and strength, always ready to help in times of trouble."*

Tapping into the wisdom of God's presence will save you a boatload of grief.

Second, I can overcome my anger/reactions...

With the Wisdom of God's Protection

"⁴A river brings joy to the city of our God, the sacred home of

the Most High. ⁵God dwells in that city; it cannot be destroyed. From the very break of day, God will protect it. ⁶The nations are in chaos, and their kingdoms crumble! God's voice thunders, and the earth melts! ⁷The LORD of Heaven's Armies is here among us; the God of Israel is our fortress" (Psalm 46:4-7)

When you get pressed in a moment of chaos or disagreement, how do you respond? This next part of our study illustrates the importance of having something deep inside you to protect you from blowing your lid. In other words, what type of river runs within the city of your soul? Who sits on the throne of your heart?

Verse five tells us that if, *"God dwells in that (your) city; it cannot be destroyed. From the very break of day, God will protect it."* There's a dual protection going on here. Not only does God protect you from your enemies from outside your borders, but here we learn that God protects you from the enemy within your borders. And most of the time your biggest enemy within your borders is you.

There are several stories in the Bible that highlight the dangers of anger and its negative consequences. Here are a few examples:

Cain and Abel in Genesis 4. Cain was angry at his brother, Abel, because God accepted Abel's offering but not Cain's. Cain's anger led him to commit the first murder, when he killed Abel. It's a reminder of the destructive power of unchecked anger deep within.

Saul's jealousy of David in 1 Samuel 18-19. Saul, the first king of Israel, became jealous and angry at David's popularity and success. His anger grew to the point where he attempted to kill David on several occasions causing him to lose his leadership as King. God withdrew His presence from Saul. It's a reminder that uncontrolled anger can lead to irrational and harmful behavior and cause us to lose the influence God wants us to have.

The Prodigal Son's older brother in Luke 15. In this parable, the older brother becomes angry and resentful when his younger brother returns home after squandering the family inheritance. The older brother's anger prevents him from rejoicing in his brother's return and strains their relationship. It's a reminder of the dangers of holding onto anger and self-righteousness, which can alienate you from others and hinder forgiveness.

These three stories emphasize the need to manage anger and its potential consequences. They remind us of the importance of self-control, forgiveness, and seeking reconciliation instead of letting anger consume us.

If I had an orange on the stage with me and I squeezed it, what would come out? Apple juice? Nope. Grapefruit juice? Nope. It would be orange juice. Why? Because it is an orange and that's what's inside.

Let's assume the orange is you. And someone squeezes you, puts pressure on you, says something you don't like or offends you. And out of you comes anger, hatred, bitterness, fear. Why? The answer is that's what's inside.

It doesn't matter who does the squeezing–your mother, your brother, your children, your boss, the government. If someone says something about you that you don't like, what comes out of you is what's inside. And what's inside is up to you. It's your choice.[38]

When you learn to manage your anger you not only improve your own life, but also contribute to making the lives of those around you better. The Bible also warns that uncontrolled anger can have negative internal consequences that you want to avoid.

"Hot-tempered people must pay the penalty." (Prov 19:19)

"Be quick to listen, slow to speak, and slow to get angry. Human anger does not produce the righteousness God desires." (James 1:19-20)

Again, that penalty is not just outside of you, it's also inside. The medical world has identified time and again that anger is not good for your health.

A recent study from a group of doctors in Coral Gables, Florida compared the effectiveness of the heart's pumping action in 18 men with coronary artery disease to nine men who were healthy. Each of the men underwent one physical stress test (riding an exercise bicycle) along with three mental stress tests: Doing math problems in their heads, recalling a recent incident that had made them very angry, and giving a short speech to defend themselves against a hypothetical charge of shoplifting.

The doctors took pictures of the subjects' hearts in action during these tests. For all the subjects, anger reduced the amount of blood that the heart pumped to body tissues more than the other tests, but this was especially true for those who had heart disease.[39]

I like this researcher's conclusion, "Why anger is so much

more potent than fear or mental stress is anybody's guess. But until we see more research on this subject, it couldn't hurt to count to 10 before you blow your stack."

What's the third way I can overcome my anger/reactions?

Third, I can overcome my anger/reactions…

With the Wisdom of God's Plan

"⁸Come, see the glorious works of the LORD: See how He brings destruction upon the world. ⁹He causes wars to end throughout the earth. He breaks the bow and snaps the spear; He burns the shields with fire. ¹⁰Be still and know that I am God! I will be honored by every nation. I will be honored throughout the world. ¹¹The LORD of Heaven's Armies is here among us; the God of Israel is our fortress." (Psalm 46:8-11)

When you get angry, do you have a plan? Most of us don't. If you're honest, you usually just let the emotion of that moment drive your decisions. Whatever happens, happens. God doesn't want you to go through life being held hostage to your anger, being held hostage to your emotions. He doesn't want you to go through life like a wrecking ball taking down the people around you. Stop doing that, it hurts.

Verse eight encourages us to look around us and *"Come, see the glorious works of the LORD."* What are those glorious works? What is it that the Bible is inviting you to see?

Here it is, the Bible is teaching us in Psalm 46:9 that God, *"causes wars to end."* He *"breaks the bow"* and *"snaps the spear"* and *"burns the shields."* This means God can bring an end to hostilities in your heart. He can cause a cease-fire within the battle of your soul. He can remove the barriers/shields you've put in place between yourself and others.

How does He do it? We find the key in verse 10, *"Be still, and know that I am God!"* Say that out loud: *"Be still and know that I am God!"* Say it again, *"Be still, and know that I am God!"*

Here is your battle plan the next time you feel anger rising up within you. Here is your strategy to overcome your situation. *"Be still and know that I am God!"*

Some of you may be asking, can God really do this? Can God really *"break the bow"* and *"snap the spear"* of anger in my heart? Can God disarm my weapons of anger? Can He cause the "war of anger" in my life to end? I think He can. Let me tell you why. Not only can I make the case through the promise of scripture, but I can make the case in my own life.

When I was growing up, one of the things that really hit me was this issue of anger. Although most of the time life was fun and exciting; I had a tough time with this issue. I would get in fights at school. I would argue with anyone about anything just to win a battle. I was very confrontational, hard-hitting, and uncompromising. You don't have to take my word for it, you can talk to my family.

My anger was so bad that when I was a kid my grandfather (who I was super close to) once told me, "If you don't get your anger under control, you're going to end up in jail by the time you're 18."

Anger Management (Ps 46)

It was true that although I had great dreams in life and talent in certain areas, I knew if I didn't get this issue under control, this hair-trigger emotion of anger would cause great damage to my life.

But something happened when I got serious about my relationship with God. When I was 16, I rededicated my life to Jesus and got serious about my faith. One of the first things that changed in my life was the ending of hostilities in my heart. It was actually shocking. I wasn't expecting it. It was just like this verse describes. God *"broke the bow"* and *"snapped the spear."* He caused the *"wars to end."*

For many of you, the reason you're fighting everyone around you is that you're fighting with God. You're fighting for control of your life. You want to be in control. You want to have the last say. You want to dictate to God and everyone else the terms of the deal. When you do that and others don't go along with you and your plan, you get angry. If you want to fix your problem with anger, fix your relationship with Jesus first.

The plan of God is simple, *"Be still and know that He is God."* And when you do that, when you surrender your entire life to Him, He will change you. He will mold you. He will turn you into a vessel that brings honor to His name instead of being a person who leaves a trail of destruction in your own name.

The funny part about this whole story for me was that shortly after I got serious in my relationship with Jesus one of the girls in my class (this was my junior year) came up to me and said, "What's up with you anyway?" And I said, "I don't know, what do you mean?" She said, "Why in the world are you always smiling? You walk around school like everything is great all the time." I remember that moment because it was the first time in my life that someone from the outside told me they noticed a difference in my demeanor. It was totally cool because I knew this type of change didn't come from me. This change in my life came from Jesus.

We shouldn't be surprised when God changes us, because the Bible promises us that's what will happen. When you come to God and ask Him to help you, when you go all in with what the Bible says, *"I will give you a new heart, and I will put a new spirit in you. I will take out your stony, stubborn heart and give you a tender, responsive heart"* (Ezekiel 36:26)

That kind of change only comes from Jesus.

God has you reading this for one of two reasons: One, if you're far away from Him, He's calling you closer. Two, if you're already close to Him, He's calling you to reach out to those around you. In either case, it's always about connecting your story with God's story. Have you done that?

We all have a story, but our story has no real meaning until we connect it to God's eternal story. And that Story, God's eternal story, is a grand story of redemption connected to the entire world. It started on day one of human history and continues to this very moment. It's a Divine Story that we have the privilege of being a part of if we humble ourselves and say, "YES, I want to serve Jesus."

Here's my challenge, some of you reading this are desperately looking for a way out of this addiction. I know it, you know it, but most importantly, God knows it. Here's what you need to do.

If you have yet to surrender your life over to Jesus, you need to start there.

He will take your life, as you are, and as you walk with Him in obedience each step of the way, He will walk you out of this addiction and into the life He has designed for you to live.

Chapter 8

From Bitterness
to Better-*ness*:
Learning to Forgive

Psalm 37

On New Year's Day, 1929, Georgia Tech played UCLA in the Rose Bowl. In that game a young man named Roy Riegels recovered a fumble for UCLA. Picking up the loose ball, he lost his direction and ran sixty-five yards toward the wrong goal line. One of his teammates ran him down and tackled him just before he scored for the opposing team. Several plays later, UCLA had to punt. Georgia Tech blocked the kick and scored a safety, demoralizing the Bruins.

At half-time the players filed into the dressing room. Riegels sat down in a corner and put his face in his hands. Coach Price was quiet. No doubt he was trying to decide what to do with Riegels. When the timekeeper came in and announced that there were three minutes before the second half, Coach Price said, "Men, the same team that played the first half will start the second." The players got up and started out, all but Riegels. The coach said, "Roy, didn't you hear me? The same team that

139

played the first half will start the second."

Riegels looked up, and said, "Coach, I can't do it. I've ruined the university's reputation. I've ruined myself. I can't face that crowd." The coach said, "Roy, get back out there. The game is only half over."

Have you ever felt like you have run the wrong way on the issue of forgiveness? Someone offended you and you picked up that offense and ran it toward the goal line of bitterness. Now you're in the locker room of regret, and you're too embarrassed to find your way out. Listen, all of us have run a long way in the wrong direction. I want to impress upon you today that the game is only half over.

The Bible teaches us two truths about forgiveness. One, God is forgiving, *"But you are a God ready to forgive, gracious and merciful, slow to anger and abounding in steadfast love."* (Nehemiah 9:17)

Two, He wants you to be as well, *"Be kind to one another, tenderhearted, forgiving one another, as God in Christ forgave you."* (Ephesians 4:32)

But how many of you know that being like God and forgiving others is a lot easier said than done? We need some help in this area, don't we?

This is an important issue because forgiveness can save you from the expense of anger and the high cost of hatred, and ultimately can break the shackles of bitterness.

So, how can you move from bitterness to better-ness? According to Psalm 37, there are three things you can do to help

140

you become a more forgiving person.

First, you can move from bitterness to better-*ness* when you...

Redirect Your Attention

"¹Don't worry about the wicked or envy those who do wrong. ²For like grass, they soon fade away. Like spring flowers, they soon wither" (Psalm 37:1-2)

There are a lot of things vying for your attention. Marketers, influencers, and political action groups are all attempting to get it. They want a commitment, a like, a follow, or a purchase. There is no shortage of attention-grabbing information out there. In fact, one recent study showed we are bombarded with hundreds of ads every day.[40] Thankfully, most of them we simply ignore.

But there's one thing that grabs your attention and is very difficult to ignore. That's when somebody offends you. It's when somebody does something wrong to you. That gets your attention every time. And then you stew on it for hours, days, weeks, and even months. Has that ever happened to you?

Maybe you've been going about your day, and then bam, somebody crisscrosses your life. Somebody "bumps you." They're rude, condescending, and disrespectful. What do you do when that happens? Most of the time you stop instantly, and all your attention is now directed at this person and the situation. Then throughout the day you tell everybody all about it. "Can you believe this happened to me?" "I mean, how rude can some people be?"

The first way to overcome resentment and begin releasing forgiveness in your life is to redirect your attention away from those who have done something against you. In other words, look past the situation. Stop focusing on it. Look how the Bible describes it, *"Don't worry about the wicked or envy those who do wrong."*

Why do you think God is telling you not to worry about those who harm you? Because you do, that's why. If this wasn't a problem, God wouldn't be telling you to stop doing it. In fact, God has to go so far as to say, don't be jealous of them as well. The Hebrew word, *envy*, is קָנָא qânâ'(kaw-naw), and it means to be jealous.

The Bible points out our natural tendency to give back what has been given to us. Meaning, I want to do what they've done. If someone hates on us, we want to hate them back. If someone is rude to us, we want to be rude back. If someone refuses to forgive us, we refuse to forgive them. And the cycle goes on and on.

This isn't a way to live a productive and joy-filled life. God has so much more for you. God wants you to be forgiving in your life.

Some people may ask why. Why does God want us to be forgiving? Why does God want me to forgive? Because it's good for you, that's why! Not only that, but we need it. In fact, 62% of American adults say they need more forgiveness in their personal lives, according to a survey by the Fetzer Institute.

Studies have found that those who are more forgiving tend to be more satisfied with their lives and have less depression, anxiety, stress, anger, and hostility. People who hang on to grudges, however, are more likely to experience severe depression and post-traumatic stress disorder, as well as other health conditions.

"There is an enormous physical burden to being hurt and disappointed," says Karen Swartz, M.D., director of the Mood Disorders Clinic at The Johns Hopkins Hospital.

Chronic anger puts you into a fight-or-flight mode, which results in numerous changes in heart rate, blood pressure, and immune response. Those changes, then, increase the risk of depression, heart disease, and diabetes, among other conditions. Forgiveness, however, calms stress levels, leading to improved health. Forgiveness can reap huge rewards for your health, lowering the risk of heart attack, improving cholesterol levels, blood pressure and sleep, reducing pain, and levels of anxiety, depression, and stress. Finally, research points to an increasing level of benefit as you age.[41]

What's all this telling you? Next time you're offended, wounded, or insulted, redirect your attention. Don't focus on the person, the action, or the effect. Remember what the Bible is teaching you in verse two, *"For like grass, they soon fade away. Like spring flowers, they soon wither."* Why focus your attention on something that's fading away? We do this all the time. We focus on the temporary while the eternal eludes us. I want to encourage you to flip that around. Focus on the eternal because the temporary is irrelevant.

Not only that, but also nothing that has been done to you can keep you from the most important thing in life, and that is having a relationship with God. The Bible reminds us, *"I am convinced that nothing can ever separate us from God's love. Neither death nor life, neither angels nor demons, neither our fears for today nor our worries about tomorrow—not even the powers of hell can separate us from God's love."* (Romans 8:38) If those who have offended you are going to fade like grass and wither like a flower, and nothing they have done can affect your walk with Jesus, then why are you focusing so much attention on them?

How did Jesus do this? He was insulted. He was disrespected. He was beaten, bruised, and even put to death. Yet He was able to get past it. How did He do it? How can we do it? *"We do this by keeping our eyes on Jesus, the Champion who initiates and perfects our faith. Because of the joy awaiting Him, He endured the cross, disregarding its shame. Now He is seated in the place of honor beside God's throne."* (Hebrews 12:2)

God's Word Translation says it this way: *"He saw the joy ahead of Him."*

When you focus on what's ahead of you, you don't have time to look behind you. Next time you're offended, wounded, or insulted, follow the example of Jesus and focus on the joy waiting for you in heaven and see if that doesn't help to refocus your attention from your problems.

Next, you can move from bitterness to better-ness when you…

Renew Your Affection

"³Trust in the LORD and do good; dwell in the land and

befriend faithfulness. ⁴Delight yourself in the LORD, and He will give you the desires of your heart. ⁵Commit your way to the LORD; trust in Him, and He will act." (Psalm 37:3-5)

Another way to move forward from an offense is to renew your affection toward God. Let's get a little background on Psalm 37. This is a psalm of wisdom, specifically a didactic, or instructional Psalm. It is written in the form of an acrostic, with each stanza starting with a successive letter of the Hebrew alphabet. It also contains elements of praise, lament, and assurance. It is a prayer for protection and deliverance and encourages trust in God to bring justice.

In terms of historical context, it was written by David while he was being pursued by King Saul. David was anointed by Samuel to be the next king of Israel, but Saul saw him as a threat and tried to kill him. During this time, David was forced to flee and hide in caves and wilderness areas. The enemy he faced was not only Saul, but also other enemies who sought to harm him. David walked the road of forgiveness during times of great persecution and oppression.

It is natural to feel hurt and angry when someone wrongs you. But as a follower of Jesus, you are called to a higher standard. Forgiveness is not always easy, but it is necessary for your spiritual growth and relationship with God. Remember, forgiveness is not condoning or excusing an offense; it is choosing to let go of bitterness, resentment, and revenge.

The Bible is filled with examples and teachings on forgiveness. Jesus Himself forgave those who crucified Him while He was hanging on the cross, *"...Jesus said, 'Father, forgive them, for they don't know what they are doing.' And the soldiers gambled for His clothes by throwing dice."* (Luke 23:34) Jesus knows what it feels like to forgive those who have wronged you.

In the parable of the unmerciful servant in Matthew 18, we see the importance of extending forgiveness to others as we have been forgiven by God, picking it up in verse 32, *"32Then the king called in the man he had forgiven and said, You evil servant! I forgave you that tremendous debt because you pleaded with me. 33Shouldn't you have mercy on your fellow servant, just as I had mercy on you?"* (Matthew 18:21-35) When you're in touch with your own sin, it's easier to forgive others of theirs. Watch out for self-righteousness. It can cause you to be harder on others than you should be.

In Colossians 3:13 we are reminded to forgive as the Lord has forgiven us, *"Make allowance for each other's faults, and forgive anyone who offends you. Remember, the Lord forgave you, so you must forgive others."* This reminds us that forgiveness is applied to all, just like God's forgiveness is available to all who receive it.

In all three of these passages, you will need to rely on your relationship with God to help you through them. Forgiveness can be difficult to offer at times, and often, it is not something you can do alone. You need a deeper well of strength to draw from.

Did you notice how David did it? He focused his attention on God and renewed his affection for God. He writes five things:

- "Trust in the LORD"

- "Dwell in the land"

- "Befriend faithfulness"

- "Delight in the LORD"

- "Commit your way to the LORD"

If you do these five things, The Bible says…

- "God will act"

- "God will give you the desires of your heart" and..

- "You will do good."

He will provide the ability to forgive as you follow His command to do so.

In other words when you set your affection on God, He will help you carry this through. When you set your affection on Jesus you become more like Him. You become less and less concerned about your rights and more and more concerned about His mission. And your part in His mission to the world. The South African pastor and author Andrew Murray put it this way.

"If our greatest need had been information, God would have sent us an educator; if our greatest need had been technology, God would have sent us a scientist; if our greatest need had been money, God would have sent us an economist; if our greatest need had been pleasure, God would have sent us an entertainer; but our greatest need was forgiveness, so God sent us a Savior."

If you want to move from bitterness to better-*ness*, renew your affection for Jesus. You'll find His desire to forgive running through your soul.

Finally, you can move from bitterness to better-*ness* when you...

Release Your Administration

"He will bring forth your righteousness as the light, and your justice as the noonday." (Psalm 37:6)

A seminary student in Chicago once faced a test of forgiveness. Although he preferred to work in some kind of ministry, the only job he could find was driving a city bus on Chicago's south side. One day a gang of tough teens got on board and refused to pay the fare. After a few days of this, the seminarian spotted a policeman on the corner, stopped the bus, and reported them. The officer made them pay, but then he got off. When the bus rounded a corner, the gang robbed the seminarian and beat him severely. He pressed charges and the gang was rounded up. They were found guilty.

When you get bumped, one of the first things you want to do is remain in control of the situation. If you were harmed in any way, you want to make sure justice is served. If possible, you want to be the one to administer that justice. You see, every time you are wronged, you will have the opportunity to oversee your response to the action. You will be the only one to control how you respond to it.

Let me ask you, what would you do in the situation of this young man? When those who have harmed you have been found guilty, how would you have responded?

The young Christian leader responded in a shocking way. As soon as the jail sentence was given, he saw their spiritual need and felt sorry for them. He asked the judge if he could serve their sentences. The gang members and the judge were dumbfounded. "It's because I forgive you," he explained. Ultimately, his request was denied, but he visited the young men in jail and led several of them to faith in Christ.

There's a great lesson here, and here it is: When you want to serve up judgment on someone else, remember God's mercy for you.

Consider this, Psalm 37:6 reminds us that just as we can count on the sun rising each day, we can count on the righteousness of Jesus covering us. Look how David puts it, *"He will bring forth your righteousness as the light."*

In the New Testament it says, *"God made the one who did not know sin to be sin for us, so that in Him we would become the righteousness of God."* (2 Corinthians 5:21, NET) Most of us know that and don't question it. We know that as we put our faith in Jesus, He puts on us His righteousness and we love that. We trust Him for this.

But look at the second part of Psalm 37:6, *"He will bring forth... your justice as the noonday."* What does that mean? That means in the same way you trust in Jesus for salvation, you need to trust in Jesus for His justice to be served. But wait a minute. What if God needs my help in overseeing His justice for my situation? I need to make sure it's done right. Listen, God will bring justice in His time and in a way that brings glory to Him, and He doesn't need your help.

If you want to move from bitterness to better-ness, you need to release your administration of God's justice over someone else's life. Trust God that He knows what He is doing.

I heard about a couple that was married for 15 years and were having more disagreements than usual. They wanted to make their marriage work and agreed on an idea that the wife had. A Fault Box. One for each of them. For one month they planned to drop a slip of paper in the others Fault Box. These boxes would provide a place to let their spouse know about their daily irritations. The wife was diligent in her efforts and approach: leaving the top off the peanut butter jar, wet towels on the shower floor, dirty socks not in the hamper, on and on until the end of the month. After dinner at the end of the month, they exchanged boxes. After reading his, the husband reflected on what he had done wrong. Then the wife opened her box and began reading each slip of paper. They were all the same. The message on each slip said, "I love you!"

You can go through life making sure everyone's getting what they deserve, or you can go through life with God's love and mercy. It's up to you. The Bible teaches us today that when you love like Jesus, forgive like Jesus, and serve like Jesus, you don't have to worry about getting back at those who've harmed you. God will take care of it as sure as lunch arrives each day, God will make sure that justice is served on those who need it.

Let me share a story about a person who lived out forgiveness in a way that transformed many lives.

In the African country of Rwanda, 1994 was a year like no other. 800,000 people were killed in an act of genocide. Soldiers from one ethnic group killed another. The scale and brutality shocked the world, but no country intervened to stop it. Gangs of soldiers searched out victims hiding in churches, school buildings, and homes.

One of the victims was a child named Jean Claud. He had grown up in a family that brought him to church and introduced him to Jesus. Tragically, he witnessed the death of his father. He watched from hiding as other family members were killed as well. This should have put an end to Jean Claud's future. But God had other plans.

Eventually, Jean Claud forgave those who killed his family. Ten years after the war, from this tragedy, he founded Best Family Rwanda for children. The children he helps are mostly from the rival group that killed his family.

But one day, his heart of forgiveness was challenged. One of the children sponsored in his organization was the son of his father's murderer. After the genocide, this child's father was imprisoned for his crime. Jean Claud said, "Bring his orphan. He doesn't have a father."

He continued, "I love that child of my father's murderer. I have supported him through high school, and he has now graduated college."

Because of his willingness to leave justice in the hands of God and to share freely from a heart of forgiveness, Jean Claud's organization has helped thousands of children from both sides of this travesty. Not only in providing a better life but ultimately in experiencing the love of Jesus.

If God can remove the anger and hatred from Jean Claud's heart, He can remove the anger from your heart. The only person who can remove the anger and bring peace, safety, and calm to your life, to your situation is Jesus. It all starts with Him.

If you have yet to give your life over to Jesus, I want to invite you to do so right now. You can't find the freedom you're looking for without Him. You can't find the forgiveness you need outside of Him. You can't connect with the true purpose for your life separated from Him.

Come to Jesus and do it today. Don't put it off. He's the only one who can heal you from your past as He restores and readies you for your future. It is time for you to connect your story with God's story.

Chapter 9

Finding Truth in a World Overflowing with Information

Psalm 119

Have you ever set out on a journey and reached a completely unrelated destination? On three different occasions, in three different corners of the world, destiny smiled upon mankind.

In a cluttered St. Louis kitchen in 1904, Richard Blechynden was battling the summer heat, attempting to promote his piping hot tea. But the sweltering temperature mocked his efforts. In a desperate attempt to lure customers, he poured the tea over ice. As the chilled liquid refreshed the throats of fairgoers, iced tea was accidentally born, and a cool revolution began.

Across the Atlantic, in 1928 Scotland, Dr. Alexander Fleming returned to his messy laboratory after a long vacation. Amidst petri dishes brimming with bacteria, he found an oddity: one dish had a mold that killed the bacteria around it. Penicillin, the world's first true antibiotic, was not a product of deliberate design, but a quirk of fate. It heralded a new era in medicine, saving countless lives.

Decades earlier, in 1856, in a French factory, chemist Sir William Perkin was in search of a cure for malaria. Instead of a medical breakthrough, he stumbled upon a vivid colored dye. The world's first synthetic dye transformed fashion overnight, making vibrant colors accessible to all.

Three unrelated discoveries, unplanned and unexpected, changed how we drink, heal, and dress. In these moments of pure chance, the world found refreshment, healing, and color.

Sometimes life works out that way. We stumble upon a great answer. In a way we could say sometimes we stumbled upon the truth. But more times than not, life isn't like that. It's more likely that when we're lost, confused, doubting, or otherwise searching to find our way through the complexities of life, we can't find the right answer. The truth eludes us. It's like that famous 1987 song from Bono and his band U2, "I still haven't found what I'm looking for."

There's never been a time in all human history where you can gain access to more information than today. With a few clicks on your phone, you can discover the opinions, thoughts, and discoveries of countless people. Some of it is good, some of it bad. Most of it is completely worthless. If you're not careful, you can burn away an entire Saturday afternoon "doom scrolling" on your smartphone.

In fact, the Information Age has coined a sarcastic phrase we all know, "Oh, you found it on the internet; well, it must be true."

The problem with all this information is that it's extremely difficult to find out what's actually true. This is important because the Bible warns us, *"Let him not put trust in worthless things, being led astray, for what he gets in exchange will prove worthless."* (Job 15:31 CSB) The stakes are high, and yet the consequence of trusting in faulty information is unavoidable.

Because of this we've learned to fact-check, double-check, and look at everything through a lens of skepticism. One of the consequences of this is the danger of becoming so skeptical or confused that you get lost in a sea of conflicting information. You can become stunned or frozen in your ability to make a solid decision. It's a place where confusion, doubt, uncertainty, and insecurity can thrive. It's a place where your fear can overtake your faith.

Furthermore, an overflow of information can create questions for us. Questions like, is truth real? How do I find the truth in my situation? Is it okay to doubt? What if my truth intersects with your truth, who's right? And more importantly, what if both of our "truths" conflict with God's truth as found in the Bible? Now what do I do?

These questions and more can derail your walk with God and can cause your heart to grow cold and your thoughts to become chaotic. God doesn't want that for you. In fact, God wants you to walk in wisdom. God wants you to know the truth. The Bible records that Jesus said to those who believed in Him, *"[31] You are truly my disciples if you remain faithful to my teaching. [32] Then you will know the truth, and the truth will set you free."* (John 8:31-32 CEB)

According to the next Top Ten psalm in the series, Psalm 119, there are three ways to overcome confusion and discover the truth.

First, you can overcome confusion because…

God's Word Brings Truth

"⁴⁹Remember Your word to your servant, in which you have made me hope. ⁵⁰This is my comfort in my affliction, that your promise gives me life." (Psalm 119:49-50)

Let's provide a little background to today's psalm. Psalm 119 is the longest chapter in the Bible. It consists of 176 verses. It's a psalm entirely devoted to the topic of God's word and its importance in the life of a believer. The psalm is divided into 22 stanzas or sections, with each section corresponding to a letter of the Hebrew alphabet. It is purposely poetic. Let us look at just one of the 22 sections, the 7th section of the psalm that includes verses 49-56.

Historically Psalm 119 was written during the time of King Hezekiah in the 8th century BC, 700 years before Jesus. This was a time of great political turmoil for the Israelites. They were constantly under threat of invasion from surrounding nations. It was written during times of struggle, trial, confusion, and doubt.

Much like our day, the people of God were living in confusing times. Yet unlike their day, the sources of our attack are not from a foreign military, but a foreign morality, a foreign ethic. What I mean by that is, for most of our national history, we upheld a basic Judeo-Christian ethic. We held a collective confidence in a set of core biblical truths.

Dr. Richard Lee writes, "America's founding fathers gave us the country's founding documents. These documents sprang from a common acceptance of what has come to be known as the Judeo-Christian Ethic. The term "Judeo-Christian" refers to "the influence of the Hebrew Bible and the New Testament on one's system of values, laws and ethical code."

As our culture has drifted further from a godly center, attacks upon the truth of God's word have continued. And they continue today. Each subsequent year the attacks get louder and strike harder. Yet we shouldn't be surprised by this. The Bible predicts in the last days the world will experience a challenge for truth and truthfulness.

Right before His final days on earth, Jesus warned, *"You will be persecuted, you will be hated, many will be led into sin, many will betray and hate each another, and false prophets will deceive many. These confusing times will lead to the love of many growing cold."* (Matthew 24:9-12).

Jesus assures us that even in the middle of this global deception and dishonesty, *"The person who endures to the end will be saved."* (Matthew 24:13 NET) Meaning that people will find and know the truth and will endure the deception, the lies, and the confusion. So, we are able to find truth even during troubling times. How do you find this truth?

Verse 14 shows us how. Jesus promises, *"This gospel of the kingdom will be preached throughout the whole inhabited earth as a testimony to all the nations, and then the end will come."* (Matthew 24:14 NET) Here's what the Bible is saying: The truth of God's word, the truth of the gospel, will not be denied, it won't be stalled out or be stopped. The story of God's love and grace for His fallen creation will be told. Nothing can stop it.

The truth of God's Word will be attacked, but those attacks will not change the truth of its message and the impact of its words, especially to those who are looking for the truth.

The psalmist says *"⁴⁹Remember your word to your servant, in which you have made me hope "⁵⁰This is my comfort in my affliction, that your promise gives me life."* (Psalm 119:49-50)

God's word brings you hope, comfort, and life! The enemy of your soul wants the opposite for you. The devil wants you to be discouraged, afflicted, and both physically and spiritually dead. Ultimately separated from God for all eternity.

This whole thing plays itself out through an ungodly culture. Culture wants you to believe that in a world of competing truth claims, you can't know what to believe. And then within the void of uncertainty, magically, the societal leaders boldly claim, "You can follow my truth." In fact, this is the way the Antichrist will come to power one day. He will assert in a confused and corrupt world that he is the ultimate source of peace and truth for the world. It will be the greatest deception of all mankind.

So, what's the answer to all of this? How can we respond? How do we protect ourselves?

We can learn from verses 49 and 50 that God's word creates hope. God's word gives life. And in affliction, you can find comfort through the promise in His Word.

Remember, God's truth will always supersede a culture. This isn't God's first rodeo. He has seen this movie before. You may live in a culture of deceit, but you follow a Savior who is above the deceit. *"He is the Way, the Truth, and the Life."* (John 14:6)

Next, you can overcome confusion because…

The Wicked Will Not Triumph

"⁵¹The insolent utterly deride me, but I do not turn away from your law. ⁵²When I think of your rules from of old, I take comfort, O LORD. ⁵³Hot indignation seizes me because of the wicked, who forsake your law." (Psalm 119:51-53)

It's easy to get fired up in a culture that's setting fires all around you. Every time you turn on the news or go online the stories of deceit, wickedness, and dishonesty never stop. Just when you think we've hit bottom as a culture, someone lowers it even further.

This was the kind of world the psalmist was living through. He describes a culture in chaos, a group of people who were blatant and disgraceful in their lifestyle and behavior. If you're not careful, you can get sucked into their whirlwind of commotion and completely miss out on what God wants to do in your life. It can clutter, confuse, and cloud your thinking, which can happen quickly too.

Did you notice the psalmist doesn't let the bad actions of others negatively affect his relationship with God? What does he do? He commits his heart to the Lord and refuses to turn away from God's Word.

How do you maintain your coolness in the midst of a chaotic world?

Finding Truth (Ps 119)

According to this passage, you can maintain your spiritual stability by doing these things...

- Don't turn away from Jesus.

- Direct your thoughts toward God.

- Control your anger toward others.

Here's the big question to consider on this point, how many followers of Jesus have lost their focus over the past few years and gone down the rabbit hole of societal indignation? Bridges have been burned down, connections have been cut off, kingdom building has been put on hold in many lives.

Is it possible that we can lose our focus (or get confused) on what truly matters as we chase after what really bothers us? I think it is. I think we can do better on this issue.

Once we understand that the wicked will not prevail, we can release our concerns and trust that God will handle those who refuse to accept Him. And He will do this in His own time.

I struggle with this one as much as you do. I see the craziness all around me, and I want to fix it. And fix it now! I grow tired of hearing and seeing our national agencies, educational institutions, corporate structures, and entertainment industries all heading in the same direction. And I think, I'm only one person, what can I do? I'm not going to riot, protest, rage, rant, or otherwise cause some public disturbance. I'm not going to make a public nuisance of myself.

I want to follow the biblical example of Romans 12:8, *"Do all that you can to live in peace with everyone."*

This matches a similar encouragement in the book of Hebrews, *"Work at living in peace with everyone, and work at living a holy life, for those who are not holy will not see the Lord."* (Hebrews 12:14) Three words pop out, *"work at living..."*

The Bible encourages us to live in peace, not to be purposefully disruptive. We're called to carry out *"a holy life."* That means living a day-to-day life that honors Jesus, and it also includes our civic duties of voting, running for office, serving on community boards, helping minister to the greater needs around us, and being a force for good in our culture.

How can we balance all of this? How can we be a different kind of people in a chaotic world?

Let's look at an example from history. In his autobiography, Benjamin Franklin described the darkness that filled the streets of Philadelphia in his day. It was pitch black at night, and people were stepping into mud puddles and stumbling over rough stones. Even worse, crime was increasing. It wasn't safe to be out after sunset. Franklin waged an intense campaign to persuade everyone to light the area outside their own house, but he got nowhere. Finally, he just did it himself, but only in front of his own house. He planted a pole in front of his porch with a kerosene light on top. That night in the city of Philadelphia, there was one house bathed in a warm glow. The lamp cast light on the street, giving passersby a feeling of well-being and safety. The next night, another house had a lamp, then another. Pretty soon, almost the whole city was lighting the walkways in front of their houses at night. Franklin learned something: our example is often greater than our admonitions and campaigns.[42]

With that in mind, look at how Paul encourages the believers in Ephesus, *"For once you were full of darkness, but now you have light from the Lord. So live as people of light!"* (Ephesians 5:8) This one little verse is short enough to memorize, but powerful enough to illuminate the pathways around your life.

Finally, you can overcome confusion because...

God Provides Wisdom for the Traveler

"[54]Your statutes have been my songs in the house of my sojourning. [55]I remember your name in the night, O LORD, and keep your law. [56]This blessing has fallen to me, that I have kept your precepts." (Psalm 119:54-56)

The Karnak temple complex in Egypt is home to some of the oldest ruins in history. One of the temples features a set of Egyptian hieroglyphics that describe the first recorded war in history. The battle took place on April 16, 1457, BC, in the Valley of Armageddon between Pharaoh Thutmose III and a large coalition of Canaanite tribes. The Egyptians won the battle and took the Canaanite's walled city, Megiddo, seven months later. Interestingly, Megiddo is not a mountain but a manmade hill that gained its height from the repeated destruction and rebuilding of the city.

Today the Valley of Armageddon is the breadbasket of Israel, producing huge amounts of crops like barley, wheat, oranges, beans, and sunflowers. The area has also seen as many as two hundred battles throughout history, making it a place of significant historical importance.

It is from this exact spot that the Antichrist will set up his base in the final war of history. (Revelation 16:16) It's fascinating to think that our planet has a land surface of more than fifty-seven million square miles, yet the first and last recorded battles were (and will be) fought in the same place. These wars serve as bookends to the history of conflict and chaos in a fallen world. In between them lies a long story of countless confusion and clashes.[43]

The sad truth of humanity is we live in a fallen world among fallen people. One day Christ will return to bring this chaos to order, but in the meantime, we live in the midst of a confused and chaotic culture. But for those who follow Christ, God has given you His Word (The Bible) and His presence (The Holy Spirit) so that you can have the wisdom to journey well through life.

Some of you need wisdom for your situation. Some of you are facing something you weren't expecting. Your heart is filled with doubt. Some of you are staring down the long tunnel of regret, and you can't seem to find the light leading you out. Your job is in jeopardy, your spouse wants a divorce, your kids are struggling, you're low on options and resources, and you're running out of time. The journey for you today is tough. It's difficult. It's bleak.

Whatever the case, the only answer to your situation is to find the wisdom of God to lead you through this. *"[55]I remember your name in the night, O LORD, and keep your law. [56]This blessing has fallen to me, that I have kept your precepts."* (Ps 119:55-56)

According to this passage, the way out is to gain wisdom from God's word. You need direction from the heart and mind of God. He will walk with you during your darkest night. The blessing of God's wisdom will fall on you as you commit to the truth of His Word.

Let me share four things about wisdom that are important for you to know.

Wisdom is available for Everyone: *"If any of you need wisdom, you should ask God, and it will be given to you."* (James 1:5 CEV) There isn't one person who will not get wisdom if they ask God for it.

Wisdom is a gift from God: *"For the LORD grants wisdom! From His mouth come knowledge and understanding."* (Proverbs 2:6) You can't buy it, trade for it, or bargain with God for it. It's a free gift, just like salvation.

Wisdom can be Seen: *"Wisdom from above is first of all pure. It is also peace loving, gentle at all times, and willing to yield to others. It is full of mercy and the fruit of good deeds. It shows no favoritism and is always sincere."* (James 3:17) You will know when you have it, and so will others. You can't fake godly wisdom.

Wisdom is a treasure found in Christ: *"²Not only is (Jesus) the key to God's mystery, ³but all wisdom and knowledge are hidden away in Him. ⁴I tell you these things to keep you from being fooled by fancy talk."* (Colossians 2:2-4 CEV) Many claim wisdom can be found outside of God, but true wisdom, godly wisdom, is only found in Jesus. The Bible says, don't be fooled, *"All wisdom and knowledge are hidden in Jesus."*

If you need wisdom today for your journey, you can find it through a personal relationship with Jesus.

David Shatto grew up going to church. But like many, when he went away to university, he had plenty of questions and lots of confusion. He remembers sitting in his dorm room when he realized that he wasn't sure what he really believed. He remembers saying to himself, "I renounce Christianity." He became an agnostic.

He then realized the plan for his life had to change. Without God, his new mission in life was to immerse himself in science and technology.

UCLA became his secular cathedral of greatness. He began working at the Institute for Geophysics and Planetary Physics. His whole life was wrapped up in learning. Years later he couldn't help but think, I've achieved everything I've wanted to, but I didn't see any real meaning for life after that. True purpose in life eluded him.

But something happened that changed his life. In May 2016, The Salvation Army had an international band celebration in Long Beach, California. He got tickets for himself and his wife.

As they attended the event, in the middle of the program, there was a soloist who sang, "It is Well with My Soul." David said, "When I heard the song, I knew my soul was not well. And that's when everything changed."

God told him, "This is what you're missing. This is what you've been looking for." His walls against God crumbled. It was an overpowering experience. His agnostic arguments came tumbling down, and he couldn't stand against his experience with an Almighty God. Since that day, his life has never been the same.

David now says to atheists and agnostics, "You're missing something. You're missing something that affects your soul. Is it well with you if your soul is not well? Only a relationship with Jesus Christ can make you well."

We began the chapter by asking, have you ever set out on a journey and reached a completely unrelated destination?

Maybe you have arrived at a place in your life where you don't know which way to turn. You are lost, frustrated, confused, or maybe at the end of your rope. It feels like there's an emptiness deep in the center of your heart.

Do you know why you feel that way? Because God made us to know Him. He made us so that we could have a relationship with Him. And if you haven't received Jesus into your life, you will continue to sense that emptiness.

You can change that. You can come to Jesus, just as you are, and He will hear your prayer and come into your life. You can begin that journey with Jesus now.

Chapter 10

Becoming Extraordinary God's Way

Psalm 1

A friend of mine was at a fundraising dinner for Children's Scripture Engagement. It was an event focused on getting God's Word into the hands of children around the world.

My friend was tasked with hosting a table at this event. He arrived early and one person was already seated at the table. He sat down next to this unassuming, ordinary guy, and they started talking. He learned about his upbringing, his schooling, and his family.

Then, he became perplexed at how such a regular guy got into a fundraising dinner tasked to raise millions of dollars for distributing God's Word to kids around the world. He finally asked what this ordinary guy did for a living. He answered, "I invent things." Have you ever invented anything I would know about? "Bottle caps," he said. "Bottle caps?" I asked. Yes, I invented the plastic twist bottle cap just like this one here. The man reached for a bottle of water in front of him and twisted off the lid.

"So, you are telling me every time someone twists off a plastic bottle cap, you make a little money?" The man smiled. God blessed an ordinary guy with an extraordinary idea that allowed him to facilitate God's Word to millions of children.

It is one thing to create an extraordinary invention, but it is a better thing to be extraordinary in your intention. In other words, don't be average in your Christian experience. Don't be ordinary as you live for God; be extraordinary.

Throughout the pages of the Bible, you run into magnificent people who did amazing things for God. People who lived extraordinary lives. Reading through these stories, you quickly discover that within each generation, it's as if God placed unique individuals to do something spectacular for His kingdom.

For example, when describing the life of Daniel, the Bible says, *"By his extraordinary spirit, Daniel distinguished himself among the administrators and satraps. So the king planned to set him over the whole kingdom."* (Daniel 6:3 BSB)

Because Daniel lived an extraordinary life, he became a leader for God in his culture.

According to Psalm 1, there are three ways you can overcome a lack of purpose or meaning and become extraordinary in your life for God. In other words, there are three ways you can get a hold of God's purpose for your life.

First…

Take a Stand

"¹Blessed is the man who walks not in the counsel of the wicked, nor stands in the way of sinners, nor sits in the seat of scoffers." (Psalm 1:1)

In his book *An Enemy Called Average*, John Mason writes, "Your least favorite color should be beige." One of his main ideas is to live life on offense, because a person who lives on defense never rises above average. He writes, "Christians are to take the initiative. A lukewarm, indecisive person is never secure regardless of his wealth, education, or position."

From the pages of the Bible to the storyline of your life, God continues to look for extraordinary people to carry out His plan for the ages. God is looking for those like Daniel, those who have an extraordinary spirit. He's looking for those who can be leaders in the middle of a lost generation.

Do we really live in a lost generation? According to a recent survey, 57% of Americans are asking, "How can I find more meaning and purpose in my life?"[44] This survey points to the fact that people are searching for true meaning and true purpose. Nobody wants to live a meaningless life. Nobody wants to live a life without purpose.

That's the reason individuals like Jordan Peterson, Andrew Tate, Ben Shapiro, and others have captured a new generation. There's a void in leadership, especially among younger men. A younger generation is hungry to learn life lessons and leadership principles and turn them into some type of larger purpose.

But the bigger biblical worldview question centers not on

how to create an extraordinary life based on individual meaning and passion, but rather how to live an extraordinary life for God. The answer, in part, is realizing you have to stand for something, or you'll fall for anything.

That's what the psalmist is saying here in verse one.

Notice how it begins by saying, *"Blessed is the man."* The word "blessed" means "happy" or that an "inward joy is theirs." This is the same word used by Jesus in Matthew five during His famous Sermon on the Mount. *"Blessed are the poor in spirit, the meek, the merciful, the pure in heart, and the peacemakers,"* for this is the way to true life, meaning, and purpose.

These principles taught by Jesus were more than just life lessons and principles of leadership. Jesus' Sermon on the Mount was revolutionary to those who heard it the first time and continues to be for those who implement its wisdom today.

The promise of Jesus is shocking. He promised those who take a stand, those who live out His message, and those who step up and lead in this new way will enjoy life at a level that is nothing short of extraordinary. The type of life you will enjoy is amazing.

Jesus said, *"the kingdom of heaven"* is yours, you *"shall be comforted, inherit the earth, be satisfied, receive mercy, see God,"* and *"be called sons of God."* And why? *"For theirs is the kingdom of heaven."* And if all that wasn't enough, Jesus promised, *"Your reward is great in Heaven."* (Matthew 5:3-12)

If you know what you believe, take a stand for what you believe in, and live that out. Jesus is saying that's the first step to finding true purpose in this life and the next!

The reverse is also true according to Psalm 1:1. Notice how the Bible continues, *"Blessed is the man who walks not in the counsel of the wicked, nor stands in the way of sinners, nor sits in the seat of scoffers."* There's a process here...Strolling, Standing, Sitting.

What's going on here? The phrase *"walks not"* is a clear indication in the text not to do what's coming next. That is to not walk in the *"counsel of the wicked,"* nor stand in *"the way of sinners,"* nor sit in *"the seat of scoffers."*

These word pictures draw our attention to the way in which we Believe, Behave, and Belong. And even more, it shows the gravitational pull of mediocrity in a person's life. Evil, sin, or lukewarmness can sneak up on you. First, it's just accepting ungodly advice, then it's just adopting its way, until eventually you inherit the worldview. You inherit the attitude, the mindset, or what the Bible calls *"the seat of scoffers."* Proverbs 3:34 reminds us that it is not a good place to be. You don't want a seat at that table.

If you want to live an extraordinary life, a life of purpose, a life of biblical leadership, the first thing you learn is to take a stand for a biblical worldview. When you do, you will find inward joy.

Next...

Find Your Purpose

"²But his delight is in the law of the LORD, and on His law, he meditates day and night. ³He is like a tree planted by streams

of water that yields its fruit in its season, and its leaf does not wither. In all that he does, he prospers." (Psalm 1:2-3)

How would you like to prosper in all that you do? What a great promise. You could call that living an extraordinary life, couldn't you?

Now that you've taken a stand, you're ready for the next step. That is to find your purpose. Some may ask, does God really have a purpose for my life? He sure does. But is that a biblical concept?

There's a fascinating verse in the Book of Acts. When the apostle Paul was preaching in the city of Antioch Pisidia (modern-day Turkey), he mentions that *"When David had served God's purpose in his own generation, he fell asleep. His body was buried with his fathers."* (Acts 13:36 BSB). This is an obvious indication that God is interested in you and I having a sense of divine purpose in our own generation. Did you know God has a divine purpose for you in this generation? He does.

In both the Old and New Testaments, we can learn a lot about God's purpose and His desire to accomplish His will through people. In Isaiah, God says, *"My purpose will stand, and all my good pleasure I will accomplish."* (Isaiah 46:10 BSB)

In Ephesians, we learn that God is *"Making known to us the mystery of His will, according to His purpose, which He set forth in Christ."* (Ephesians 1:9)

In fact, the Bible teaches us that God is looking for those who are committed to Him, *"For the eyes of the LORD move to and fro throughout the earth so that He may support those whose heart is completely His."* (2 Chronicles 16:9 AMP) Do you want the support of God in your life? Is your heart completely his?

In his book, *Don't Waste Your Life*, John Piper writes, "God created us to live with a single passion to joyfully display His supreme excellence in all the spheres of life. The wasted life is the life without this passion. God calls us to pray and think and dream and plan and work not to be made much of, but to make much of Him in every part of our lives."

Do you want to know how not to waste your life?

Here, we find descriptions of a person whose life is focused on God. It's a description of a person living a purpose-filled life. The passage shows us that they enjoy and meditate on God's Word, which causes deep and godly roots in their life. This yields healthy fruit which can be sustained for a lifetime. All of this is summarized, *"In all that he does, he prospers."*

If you ever get lost in life, if you ever lose your way, all you have to do is remember Psalm 1:2-3. This passage shows you what it means to live out God's purpose.

Now, let's go a little deeper. It's been said before that the two most important days in a person's life are being born and discovering why you were born. I assume you understand the answer to the first part…being born. But what about the second part, why were you born? Many people get this second part wrong, even some Christians. Let me explain.

We get our gifts, talents, and abilities confused with our God-given purpose. God gives us certain capabilities or skills, but those things in and of themselves are not our purpose. Those abilities or talents are just the tools God gives us. We utilize those tools to live out the purposes of God in our lives.

What I've learned over the years is that we tend to focus on programs over people. Or we look to one-time events instead of an overall process. We tend to focus on our story and forget life is about connecting to God's story. Listen, we're not the main character in the story of God. He is, and we're just role players.

Here's how the Bible describes it, *"You are a chosen people. You are royal priests, a holy nation, God's very own possession. As a result, you can show others the goodness of God, for He called you out of the darkness into His wonderful light."* (1 Peter 2:9)

Your purpose is connected to a person. His name is Jesus.

Your purpose is about people. It's not programs or projects.

Your purpose is a process. That means waking up every day and simply doing the next right thing. When you do that, you become *"Like a tree planted by streams of water that yields its fruit in its season, and its leaf does not wither."*

That's your purpose!

Some people ask, how did you get to where you are? How did you get some of the things done in life that you've gotten done? I wake up each day and try to focus on doing the next right thing for that day. And when you link a bunch of those days together, a bunch of those weeks, months, and years, the next thing you know, you look back and wow, what a journey. And you can then say, "I guess that was God's purpose in my life." As I focus on Him and glorify Him, God has a way of making sure I'm in the right spot and doing the right things for His Kingdom.

Finally, if you want to live an extraordinary life, a life of purpose, a life of biblical leadership, the final thing you can do is…

Consider The Future

"⁴The wicked are not so but are like chaff that the wind drives away. ⁵Therefore the wicked will not stand in the judgment, nor sinners in the congregation of the righteous; ⁶for the LORD knows the way of the righteous, but the way of the wicked will perish." (Psalm1:4-6)

The last part of today's passage considers the future. What happens to us at the end of time? What happens to you at the end of your life on this planet? What happens to those who follow Jesus? What happens to those who choose not to follow Him? These three small verses (vs. 4-6) pack powerful meaning to every person who reads or hears them. And it's all connected to our study today on this idea of finding purpose in life.

Simply put, if dying is meaningless, then life would be meaningless too. The only reason there is purpose in this life is because we have purpose in the life to come.

Paul addresses this issue to the new believers in the city of Corinth. He asks, *"What value was there in fighting wild beasts—those people of Ephesus—if there will be no resurrection from the dead? And if there is no resurrection, "Let's feast and drink, for tomorrow we die!"* (1 Corinthians 15:32)

Without the hope of resurrection, Paul would live like the

philosophers of his day known as the Epicureans. They lived life unrestrained since they were convinced nothing came after. Today we would say, YOLO, You Only Live Once. Paul quotes from Isaiah 22:13 to capture this worldview, *"Let us eat and drink, for tomorrow we die."*

The problem with this worldview is twofold. If it's fully followed, meaning if you really lived it out to its fullest sense, you'll either end up in a Hedonistic form of living or in complete Nihilism. Both of those realities are empty, shallow, and devoid of life.

From the biblical perspective, we consider a future with God because God first considered a future with us. Look at how the Bible explains it, *"[11]It's in Christ that we find out who we are and what we are living for. Long before we first heard of Christ...He had His eye on us, had designs on us for glorious living, [12]part of the overall purpose He is working out in everything and everyone."* (Ephesians 1:11-12 MSG)

Someone may say, well, big deal, how does thinking about a better future impact my life today? Let me share with you how it does. When I focus on the future, it influences my present in three ways.

It Changes My Values

"I once thought these things were valuable, but now I consider them worthless because of what Christ has done." (Philippians 3:7) When you start to see beyond the present moment and understand that life is more than just the here and now, you begin to live differently. You start to live with an awareness that what you do now is important for your future

beyond this life. This perspective changes the way you approach every relationship, every task, and every situation. Suddenly, things that seemed so important before will appear trivial and unworthy of your attention. The closer you get to God, the smaller everything else looks.

It Changes My View

"What God has planned for people who love Him is more than eyes have seen or ears have heard. It has never even entered our minds!" (1 Corinthians 2:9 CEV) One of the biggest problems of modern life is that people tend to focus too much on short-term living. To really live a purposeful life, it's important to keep the idea of eternity in your mind and in your heart. Life is about more than just what's happening right now. Today is just the tip of the iceberg, and there's so much more underneath the surface. We can't even begin to imagine what eternity with God might be like. It's like trying to explain the internet to a mosquito. There are no words to describe something so amazing and awe-inspiring as Heaven.

It Changes My Vision

"[God's] plans endure forever; His purposes last eternally." (Psalm 33:11 GNT)

When you start thinking about the bigger picture of life, your perspective changes. You become more mindful about how you spend your time and money, and you start valuing relationships and character over fame, wealth, achievements, or even entertainment. Your priorities shift, and you realize that keeping up with trends, fashion, and popular culture is no longer important.

God has a special purpose for your life, not only while you're on earth, but for all eternity. Just like the time you spent in your mother's womb was preparing you for life outside, this life is preparing you for what comes next.

If you believe in God through Jesus, you don't have to be afraid of death. It's simply a doorway to a new beginning that lasts forever. "It will be the last hour of your time on earth, but it won't be the last of you. Rather than being the end of your life, it will be your birthday into eternal life."[45]

Let me share a story about an ordinary guy who God used to do something extraordinary with his life. When Pearl Harbor was attacked in December of 1941, a skinny shipyard worker named Desmond Dawes was among the many people in America who volunteered to serve his country. He was a follower of Christ, but he had sworn never to take a human life however, he enlisted anyway. He enlisted as a medic and resolved to step out onto the battlefield without a weapon, not even bringing a knife.

His unit was deployed to Okinawa, where they were charged with the almost impossible task of scaling a 400-foot cliff and then taking it from Japanese forces that were embedded at the top. A fierce firefight lasted the entire day. By the end of the day, they were driven back down the 400-foot cliff. There were many wounded American forces still at the top, and the only one left with the injured American soldiers was little Desmond Dawes.

As U.S forces regrouped down at the base of the cliff, suddenly they saw a body appear that was lowered by rope down the cliff. It was a wounded soldier, and then it happened again, and then it happened again, and again and again. Slowly, it became clear that the ordinary Desmond Dawes was doing something extraordinary. He stayed on top of that cliff and would sneak through enemy fire to rescue injured people and lower them one by one down the cliff. The Army estimated that Desmond Dawes had personally saved 75 men that day.

He received the Medal of Honor for his actions, and he was asked what was going through his mind as he continued to put himself in harm's way to rescue those who were hurting. Desmond said, "I just kept praying, please God, help me save one more. Please God help me save one more."

Conclusion

"Singing is a complex act," according to Sean Hutchins, lead author of a study on singing and a postdoctoral researcher at the International Laboratory for Brain, Music and Sound Research at the University of Montreal. Their studies show that 40-60% of people are poor singers. But did you know that according to a Canadian study, 98.5% of the population can be taught to sing? Isn't that interesting? I wonder how many of us are afraid to sing because we fear that we will be embarrassed by our lack of ability?

But we have learned that music isn't just about pitch and intonation. And it isn't just about who has the best sounding voice or a catchy beat. Music is about maintaining harmony in our lives. It is about cultivating an inner climate that allows us to live in the flow.

Let me ask you a question: What recurring emotions are you dealing with in your life? We have seen that God has a ready response to any situation you are facing and any mindset you have. The only thing that needs to happen to apply His responses is to plug in to God's playlist. As important as it is to know that God can meet all of our needs according to His own riches, to know that His benefits are amazing, that isn't quite enough. The goal here isn't just to change the music of our soul by incorporating God's promises into our lives. It is about inviting the presence of God to be with us and to enter into His presence.

Conclusion

Ultimately the most fantastic news I can give you is not that God can change your life by what He offers, but by who He is and how knowing Him and walking with Him is the real purpose of life. What does that look like?

There is a popular expression, "Fake it 'til you make it." In Romans 13:14, the apostle Paul instructs believers to *"put on the Lord Jesus Christ, and make no provision for the flesh, to gratify its desires."* In other words, instead of putting on a false self, put on Jesus. Put on truth and let it into your life. That's the choice that influences what our own playlist looks like because it guides us in determining what we focus on each day.

Paul paints a vivid picture of moving into the new life in Christ as trading the darkness of night for the light of day. The expression "put on Christ" occurs again in Galatians 3:27: *"For as many of you as were baptized into Christ have put on Christ."*. As in Romans 13, putting on Christ here speaks of having clothed ourselves with the new nature; believers are taught *"to put on the new self, created to be like God in true righteousness and holiness."* (Ephesians 4:24)

Speaking of playlists, the Bible says that God has *"put a new song in our mouth, a song of praise to our God."* (Psalm 40:3). And that song causes others to *"see, fear and put their trust in the LORD."*

So, there is already a song in your heart. Did you know that? The song in your heart celebrates what you consider worthy of celebration. The song of your heart is that in which your soul finds satisfaction. This is where the void in us that breeds fear, negativity, hopelessness and all the "minus" emotions is

182

replaced with a song. A hopeful song, a positive song, a song of faith and a celebratory song.

Sadly, billions engage those things that starve their souls and drive them further away from the redemptive path God has for them. It's important to note that this God song in our hearts was put there. We didn't put it there, God did. And the Bible says that it is a new song, not an old one. It's our song, written for us, for our journey, the divine song track of our unique lives.

A study by AARP (formerly the American Association of Retired Persons) found that music affects your well-being, learning, cognitive function, quality of life, and even happiness. The study found that:

Music listeners had higher scores for mental well-being and slightly reduced levels of anxiety and depression compared to people overall.

Of survey respondents who currently go to musical performances, 69% rated their brain health as "excellent" or "very good," compared to 58% for those who went in the past and 52% for those who never attended.

Of those who reported often being exposed to music as a child, 68% rated their ability to learn new things as "excellent" or "very good," compared to 50% of those who were not exposed to music.

Active musical engagement, including those over age 50, was associated with higher rates of happiness and good cognitive function.

Adults with no early music exposure but who currently

engage in some music appreciation show above average mental well-being scores.[46]

So, we can see that music itself has an impact on our mind. Couple that with the truth of God's word and you can see that the big emotional challenges we face can be overcome by listening to a song and singing it out as an act of worship.

In this book we have seen that God's playlist draws us into the presence of God. Why is that so important? Because the emotional challenges we face – anger, bitterness, anxiety, depression, fear and stress are really symptoms of the absence of God in a particular moment. And through music, by humming our way to victory, these emotions can be redirected. Anger can become a righteous response to injustice. Bitterness can become better-*ness* as we learn from injustice and use our experience to power new and healthy responses.

Anxiety can become a confession of our limitations and God's unlimited ability. Depression can become the acknowledgement of our human inability to respond and an invitation for God to step in. Stress can become creative energy pointed outward instead of stomach-churning apprehension.

We talked about truth earlier. Some years ago, there was a bestselling book titled, *Telling Yourself the Truth* by William Backus and Marie Chapian. The tagline of the book was, "Find your way out of depression, anxiety, fear, anger, and other common problems by applying the principles of Misbelief Therapy. Learn how to handle emotions properly."

This is what happens when we start walking with God. In our thinking, through our self-talk, through our communication with others, we become truth tellers. The negative emotions that sadly become songs themselves are dealt with in the light of truth. And by telling ourselves the truth, we begin to function the way God intended for us to live, and we want to share what works with others.

There's a fancy word for that called, "evangelism." That just involves sharing our story with others (our testimony) and sharing the story of Jesus. Whether we do it by speaking, singing, or living out loud.

So, what's on your playlist? What songs, what stories you tell yourself have outlived their usefulness? What needs to be deleted and what are your next uploads going to be? The Bible says in 2 Corinthians 10:5, *"We demolish arguments and every pretension that sets itself up against the knowledge of God, and we take captive every thought to make it obedient to Christ."* (NIV)

The Bible uses different metaphors to describe life. One of those metaphors is that of a battle. There's a fascinating story in the Old Testament about a time when Israel was going to war.

In 2 Chronicles 20:21 it says, *"After consulting the people, Jehoshaphat (King of Judah) appointed men to sing to the LORD and to praise Him for the splendor of His holiness as they went out at the head of the army, saying: 'Give thanks to the LORD, for His love endures forever.'"* (NIV)

In other words, the Israelites went into battle singing. And so do we. We go into the battles of our lives singing because victory is something we see in our hearts before it materializes in our lives.

Conclusion

As we have read about God's playlist, I want you to know that the deepest longings you feel can be met in the assurances God provides. Whether your song is a celebration or a lament. Whether you are giddy and ready to shout or grieving and lost in the pain of your life, know that the music of God can soothe your soul and that weeping may endure for a night, but joy – and singing – will come again in the morning. As someone said about life, there are high notes and low notes, but it is a beautiful story just the same.

About the Author

 T.K. Anderson is Lead Pastor of Compass Church in Monterey County, California. Compass has three campuses and a growing Online and TV ministry. He has served in full-time ministry for over two decades. His passion is to pastor through strong biblical teaching and writing and has a master's degree in Christian Apologetics from Biola University. He is currently completing his D.Min. degree at Southern California Seminary. He is the author of multiple books including *God 3:16 - Ten Ways God Shows His Love.* He and his wife, Dee, have three children.

Notes

[1] C.S. Lewis, Reflections on the Psalms (New York: Mariner Books, 1961), 10.

[2] J. Anderson, 'Introductory Notice' in *Joshua, Psalms 1-35* by John Calvin, Calvin's Commentaries 4, reprint edn (Grand Rapids: Baker Books, 1981), p. vi.

[3] Tremper Longmann III, Psalms (Downers Grove: IVP Academic, 2014), 47.

[4] Google analytics search from 2019-2023 in America

[5] Matt Mason, *Christ-Centered Exposition Commentary: Exalting Jesus in Psalms 51-100* (Nashville: B&H Pub, 2020), 394.

[6] Allen P. Ross, *A Commentary on the Psalms Vol. 3* (Grand Rapids: Kregel Academics, 2016), 51.

[7] Derek Kidner, *Psalms 73-150* (Downers Grove: IVP Academic, 2008), 364.

[8] Allen P. Ross, *A Commentary on the Psalms Vol. 3* (Grand Rapids: Kregel Academics, 2016), 58.

[9] John Maxwell, The 16 Undeniable Laws of Communication (Maxwell Leadership Publishing, 2023), 30.

[10] https://www.psychologytoday.com/us/blog/time-out/201707/american-anxiety, Accessed Sept 12, 2023.

[11] Tim Keller, YouTube, *Discovering How to Pray: Prayer in the Psalms*, accessed September 12, 2023.

[12] Thomas G. Selby, *The Divine Craftsman*, 175.

[13] https://en.wikipedia.org/wiki/International_Atomic_Time, accessed September 12, 2023.

[14] Briggs, *Psalms*, 209.

[15] Chen KW, Berger CC, Manheimer E, et al. Meditative therapies for reducing anxiety: a systematic review and meta-analysis of randomized controlled trials. Depress Anxiety. 2012;29(7):545-62. doi:10.1002/da.21964

[16] https://www.verywellmind.com/mindfulness-meditation-exercise-for-anxiety-2584081 Accessed September 13, 2023

[17] Randy Alcorn, *Heaven: A Comprehensive Guide to Everything the Bible Says About Our Eternal Home.*

[18] Randy Alcorn, *Heaven: A Comprehensive Guide to Everything the Bible Says About Our Eternal Home.*

[19] https://www.forbes.com/health/mind/depression-statistics/

[20] *Spurgeon at his Best* Compiled by Tom Carter, pp. 55-56.

[21] https://www.nimh.nih.gov/health/statistics/major-depression

[22] Victor Hugo

[23] https://www.apa.org/news/press/releases/2022/10/multiple-stressors-no-function

[24] Genesis 14:19, 2 Chronicles 2:12, Psalm 115:15, Psalm 121:2, Psalm 124:8, Psalm 134:3, Psalm 146:6, Acts 4:24, Acts 14:15, Revelation 14:7

[25] Max Lucado, in his book *In the Eye of the Storm*

[26] https://www.psychologytoday.com/intl/blog/the-case-connection/202208/3-things-making-gen-z-the-loneliest-generation

[27] https://www.npr.org/2023/05/02/1173418268/loneliness-connection-mental-health-dementia-surgeon-general

[28] https://www.psychologytoday.com/intl/blog/the-case-connection/202208/3-things-making-gen-z-the-loneliest-generation

[29] James White, *Meet Generation Z* (Grand Rapids, Baker Books, 2017) 65.

[30] https://en.wikipedia.org/wiki/James_Harrison_(blood_donor)

[31] https://www.hhs.gov/about/news/2023/01/04/samhsa-announces-national-survey-drug-use-health-results-detailing-mental-illness-substance-use-levels-2021.html

[32] https://drugabusestatistics.org

[33] https://www.addictiongroup.org/addiction/statistics/

[34] https://www.asicrecoveryservices.com/post/complete-list-of-all-types-of-addictions

[35] https://www.apa.org/topics/anger/control

[36] https://www.thezebra.com/resources/research/road-rage-statistics/

[37] Pritchard, James B. ed., Ancient Near Eastern Texts, 2nd ed. (Princeton, New Jersey: Princeton University Press, 1955), 287ff". Archived from the original on 2014-10-06. Retrieved 2013-07-15.

[38] https://www.beaconsofchange.com/wayne-dyers-orange-story-self-care/

[39] Spokesman-Review July 29, 1993, p. D3.

[40] https://www.thedrum.com/news/2023/05/03/how-many-ads-do-we-really-see-day-spoiler-it-s-not-10000

[41] https://www.hopkinsmedicine.org/health/wellness-and-prevention/forgiveness-your-health-depends-on-it

[42] David Jeremiah, *Where Do We Go From Here* (Thomas Nelson, 2021), 126.

[43] Jeremiah, *Where do we go from here*, 49.

[44] https://research.lifeway.com/2021/04/06/americans-views-of-lifes-meaning-and-purpose-are-changing/

[45] Rick Warren, *Purpose Driven Life* (Zondervan, 2002), 40.

[46] Andrew E. Budson, M. (2020) Why is music good for the brain?, Harvard Health. Available at: https://www.health.harvard.edu/blog/why-is-music-good-for-the-brain-2020100721062 (Accessed: 01 February 2024).

Made in the USA
Middletown, DE
17 May 2024